Comings and Goings

Comings and Goings

University Students in Canadian Society, 1854–1973

CHARLES MORDEN LEVI

McGill-Queen's University Press
Montreal & Kingston · London · Ithaca

© McGill-Queen's University Press 2003
ISBN 0-7735-2442-8

Legal deposit first quarter 2003
Bibliothèque nationale du Québec

Printed in Canada on acid-free paper that is 100% ancient forest free
(100% post-consumer recycled), processed chlorine free.

This book has been published with the help of a grant from the Humanities
and Social Sciences Federation of Canada, using funds provided by the
Social Sciences and Humanities Research Council of Canada.
The University College Literary and Athletic Society, University College
Alumni Association, and Principal's Office of University College have also
generously contributed to the publication of this book.

McGill-Queen's University Press acknowledges the financial support of
the Government of Canada through the Book Publishing Industry
Development Program (BPIDP) for its publishing activities. We also
acknowledge the support of the Canada Council for the Arts for our
publishing program.

National Library of Canada Cataloguing in Publication

Levi, Charles Morden, 1970–
    Comings and goings: university students in Canadian society, 1854–1973 /
    Charles Morden Levi.
    Includes bibliographical references and index.
    ISBN 0-7735-2442-8
    1. University College (Toronto, Ont.) – Students – Societies, etc. – History.
    1. Title
    LE3.T668L49 2003   378.1′983′09713541   C2002-902182-0

Typeset in Sabon 10/12
by Caractéra inc., Quebec City

To Neil McLean,
Teacher, Historian, and Mentor

Contents

Acknowledgments

This book began as a dissertation at York University, and I thank my supervisor, Paul Axelrod, and the other committee members, Bettina Bradbury, Gordon Darroch, Michiel Horn, Viv Nelles, Keith Walden, and William Westfall. In converting the dissertation to a book I have relied on their comments as well as those of other scholars, including Bill Bruneau, Bob Gidney, Wyn Millar, Alison Prentice, and Ruby Heap. Thanks are also due to the insightful people at the Canadian History of Education Association's early career table, especially Sara Burke and Catherine Gidney. Their insights have made my work much better than it otherwise would have been; any errors that remain are my own.

Those who sustain are as important as those who teach. Martin Friedland allowed me to work for him on the University of Toronto History Project during the preparation of this manuscript, and Ontario March of Dimes provided me with a day job while I completed the final touches at night.

I have also benefited from the continuing support of the Serial Diners of Greater Toronto and especially of Hope Leibowitz – words cannot express how valuable her companionship has been to me.

Special thanks are due to the University of Toronto Archives, especially Garron Wells and Harold Averill, who handled my endless requests for obscure and rarely retrieved materials with humour and style.

The University College Literary Society supported my early work on this project, and the college itself provided a Harcourt Brown Travel Scholarship that allowed me to complete research in the United States.

Finally, I must acknowledge the work of many archivists, independent scholars, and genealogists across North America who responded to individual requests with speed and good humour. In many cases, they were able to turn up obscure press clippings from regional newspapers that filled in what I expected would remain lacunae. I would also like to thank David Keane, who allowed me full access to his notes and cards on early graduates of Canadian universities. I hope that this work adequately continues Dr Keane's pioneering effort.

Introduction

Each year, thousands of young Canadians graduate from university. Although the group is diverse, they all share two essential things. Each student came to university from somewhere, and each of them will go somewhere after graduation. This certainty of origin and destination has been the case for every university student since the institution was first created.

Twenty years ago, students were virtually invisible in the history of Canadian higher education. This is no longer the case. A growing number of Canadian social and educational historians have returned the student to the story of Canadian universities, and it is now impossible to write the history of post-secondary institutions or programs without some understanding of the people they were expected to educate.

In this institutional focus, however, the place of the university in students' life stories has been less clear. Although much is now known about the student experience and how it related to both the curriculum and to extracurricular pursuits, less is known about the lives of students before and after their university days. Many historians have tackled this question in small portions, looking at the experiences of certain groups (most commonly women) over discrete periods of time and single institutions.[1] One scholar has performed the useful task of studying the entirety of the student experience in English Canada during the 1930s.[2]

The effect of all of this work in stimulating interest in students is undeniable. The greater historiography, however, has not assimilated these data into a complete picture of higher education. To give one example, a recent monograph on the history of the university in Ontario society makes no mention of the impact of university graduates on overall provincial development.[3] For all the research that has been done on students, the impact of the university on society as a whole is still seen as best understood by examining the role university professors occupy in moulding thought and identity. The concept that students might have an idea of their future that has nothing to do with the aims or goals of the professoriate (a perspective which comes naturally to many undergraduates) is not as yet reflected in the historiography of higher education.

Comings and Goings is an effort to make students the centre of the story by focussing on those parts of their experience that do not take place in the classroom. The protagonists are the 1,876 former officers of the Literary and Athletic Society (Lit.) of University College at the University of Toronto, from 1854 to 1973. Folded into the study are the organization's predecessor, the Literary and Scientific Socity (also known as the "Lit."), and the parallel women's groups, the Women's Literary Society (WLS) and its successor the Women's Undergraduate Association (WUA). After briefly surveying the activities of the Lit. over this nearly 120-year period, I turn to my main concern: a detailed study of the origins and future careers of its student leaders.

For each of the four cohorts I examine, I situate the students not in the context of the university they were studying at, but in relation to society as a whole. In each era, University College students were broadly representative of the society from which they came, although certain categories and classes were always more likely to attend the institution. As graduates, they entered a variety of careers and had an impact on society not entirely predicted by the university that educated them. I also explore the differing experiences of men and women in the context of the gender norms of each period, especially with regard to the often forgotten role of marriage in the lives of educated Canadian women.

From 1854 to 1973, student experiences reflected the simultaneous forces of social expansion and institutional contraction. During this period the available career choices for university students expanded as Canada became a more complex society. University College, meanwhile, contracted from a national institution serving an entire country to a parochial institution educating Toronto-born students to take roles in the evolution of their city.

Although the group studied is small and the sample is not random, the chapters that follow provide a representation of the dynamic role University College played within Canadian society over more than a century. The comings and goings of young Canadians emerge as significant factors in the general history of the country, and integral parts of the social history of higher education.

Comings and Goings

1 A Short History of the Literary and Athletic Society

The idea of founding a society for the students of University College seems to have been present from the inception of the college as a separate entity from the University of Toronto. University College was created by act of parliament in 1853, and in that summer or fall students began a "movement for the establishment of a debating society."[1]

By forming such a society, students at University College were fitting into a transatlantic story that first began in Scotland in the eighteenth century,[2] and was carried to the rest of the British Isles and the United States in the late eighteenth and early nineteenth centuries. In the United States especially, such societies had been dedicated to the development of oratory, in its older meaning of the cultivation of all aspects of the life of letters, including speaking, writing, and poetry.[3]

The Literary and Scientific Society of University College (as it was first known) had similar objectives as the Scottish, English, and American student societies, namely "the encouragement of Literary and Scientific pursuits among its members, by Discussions and Essays, on subjects suitable to that purpose, and by the establishment of a Reading Room."[4] These activities formed the backbone of Enlightenment *belles lettres* and rhetoric, and were thought to provide the "ideal education for the man of letters."[5] The Lit.'s constitution encouraged this focus by declaring that "no controverted point in religion or politics shall be admitted for discussion in the Society" at its regular Friday night meetings.[6]

The Lit. was intended to be a training ground for gentlemen. It offered members the opportunity to debate and to criticize each other's thoughts and arguments without recourse to insult or foul play. As one former officer of the Lit. declared in 1886, "It is not the book worm or medalist that has come to the front in life, but rather the member of the Literary Society who stood first in debates, who learned to amend a constitution, or to manage an election contest ... let the coming man of the world, who must know men in order to prove a peer among them, seek every chance of so doing."[7]

Apart from the general knowledge of men gained from participating in essay writing, readings, and debates, the Lit. also attempted to instill knowledge of society through its annual Conversazione, begun in 1864. The Conversazione was an evening of music, food, scientific display, and public lecture open to the whole university and to the community at large, with the only limits being a maximum attendance of 1,500 and a prohibition on dancing (not lifted until 1896).[8]

The activities of the Lit. were often criticized in the wider college community. For example, the "closed debates," with their fixed debaters and set time limits, as well as restrictions on what subjects could be debated, were often disparaged.[9] For a two-year period, younger undergraduates seized on these limitations and created the Forum, which in 1883 and 1884 held meetings off-campus and considered political topics in open debate.[10] The Forum was one of the short-lived examples of a number of specialized societies that sprang up as rivals to the Lit. The Mathematical and Physical Society, the Natural Science Association, and the Modern Languages Club, to give only the more successful examples, carried on activities that for some seemed to be more relevant to the actual needs of University College students. As one correspondent stated in 1886, "they bear more directly on the work in hand, and the work, moreover, which is most at heart: they give more opportunities to individual talent and aspirations; and they have enlisted the heavy sympathy and valuable co-operation of the professors, who have ever been conspicuous in the Literary Society by their absence."[11]

The Lit. also became a battleground for rival political factions. Elections were heavily contested and party platforms and violent polling were increasingly prevalent in the 1880s and 1890s. In 1887 one acid-tongued correspondent accused the Lit. of having gone too far in election rowdyism and partisanship, asking "Whether we are to have an election for the Society, or a Society for the elections?"[12] The strange circumstance by which an organization designed to train gentlemen to get along with each other had declined into a haven for rabble-rousers may have been exaggerated for effect by opponents of the Lit. These critics declared, however, that if University College students could not maintain a society in which high-toned debate and gentlemanly conduct were respected, then they were prepared to abandon, and possibly destroy, the organization. The Lit.'s opponents wished to have the right to debate Canadian politics in their meetings, but they did not want their elections to resemble the riots on the Ontario hustings – such was beneath the dignity of a state college.[13]

Ironically, what saved the Lit. from disaster were the external political forces that the society was indirectly aping. In 1904 the University College Council announced that it had consented to allow the Lit. to discuss any questions, even those bearing on Canadian party politics.[14] Around the same time, the Lit. introduced the secret ballot and abandoned the practice of holding "scraps," in which the outcome of an election was decided by "Brute Force" preventing voters from reaching the polls.[15]

These changes were contemporary with observations by provincial politicians that there was a lack of university-trained men in Canadian political life. The Hon. George W. Ross, premier of Ontario, declared that the university man had an obligation to join the political field, because "the only return the State gets for the vast expenditure on education is in the better equipment of its citizens ... for those higher spheres of life upon the efficiency and intelligence of which the State depends."[16] This position had its detractors, most vocal of whom was the principal of University College, Maurice Hutton, who said university students were already overtrained in politics and that political corruption in Ontario was "only the product of the reckless exuberance of youth, prolonged abnormally into maturer life."[17]

During the early years of the twentieth century, the Lit. began to change its methods of operation to better reflect the needs of university graduates in later political life. In 1908/09 one of the factions, the Old Lit. party, campaigned for office on a platform of introducing cabinet government to the running of the society. In the fall of 1910 this was finally achieved, and responsible government arrived at University College. The Lit. could now discuss political issues freely, organized on parliamentary principles. In January 1912, for the first time in the history of the organization, an executive changed in the middle of the year when the Old Lit. party was defeated on a budgetary item.[18]

In January 1913 a referendum passed, 223 to 114, allowing the Lit. to be organized along Canadian party lines. The administration of the university immediately criticized the decision, but Premier Sir James Whitney, whose province was generously funding the university, declared that it made no difference to him. The move to party politics had some immediate benefits, as politicians came to the university in greater numbers to talk to the students. This new trend culminated in an address by former prime minister Sir Wilfrid Laurier to the entire student body in December 1913.[19]

The long-term effects of the change were, however, negative, as interest in the Lit. dwindled to a committed few. In January 1915, when the Liberal party was defeated by a vote of 28 to 27 in what was described as the "Most Exciting Meeting for Years," it was obvious that the attendance of 55 was not a good sign of prosperity for the organization.[20]

The Lit.'s decline was exacerbated by the First World War. Although attempts were made to keep the executive intact, by the fall of 1916 the society was effectively defunct. Efforts were made to revive it in 1919 on the basis of political parties and parliamentary procedure, but the Lit. was reported in March 1920 to be "struggling wearily along" with almost no attendance at its meetings.[21] In the fall of 1920 this decay led to a fundamental restructuring of the organization designed to remove its specialized focus on politics and to make it a more social organization better suited to serving the entire college. As well as a new structure and orientation, there was also an urgent need for a compulsory fee to be paid by all undergraduates.

The Literary and Scientific Society of University College held its last meeting on 8 March 1921, and the Literary and Athletic Society, with compulsory fees, was established in its place.[22] This new organization was intended to continue to have debating as a main activity. By the mid-1930s, however, two other organizations, Hart House and the University College Parliamentary Club, had supplanted the Lit. as the main centres for debating on campus. The last formal debate held at an open meeting of the Lit. occurred on 4 December 1934,[23] with the exception of the annual prize debate for the Robinette Shield that continued into the 1950s.

The reinvented Lit. moved into a new role: coordinating "all the various activities and interests of the college."[24] This included the establishment, in 1926, of a University College magazine, eventually known as the *Undergraduate*, the creation of the University College *Follies* (a collection of student-written sketches performed annually), and, perhaps most important, the holding of dances.

Supervising these activities made the Lit. more of an administrative organization than it had been in the past, and occasional crises highlighted how these new initiatives superceded all other society functions. In 1925 the discovery of twenty-three forged tickets to the *Follies* delayed debate over the amalgamation of the Canadian National Railway and the Canadian Pacific Railway while the Lit. struggled to identify the forgers and prevent further such occurrences.[25] Similarly, in 1938 the discovery of discrepancies in the *Follies*' accounts delayed by at least an hour a guest speaker's address to the society.[26]

The administration of dances could also inflame opinions at University College. Throughout the late 1940s and early 1950s, the continuing question of whether to hold the annual Arts Ball, whether it should be formal or semi-formal, and whether the Lit. could afford to hire a band, took up an ever-increasing amount of time at meetings.[27]

As well, the administration of student areas caused problems. In 1924 the re-allocation of university space after the building of Simcoe Hall provided the society with a new Junior Common Room (JCR). While it welcomed the acquisition of the JCR, the Lit. was continually perplexed by how to keep the space clean and usable by students. As early as 1930 the issue of "abuse of equipment" in the JCR led to discussions about whether access to the room should be restricted.[28] Instead of taking this route, the Lit. continued to add equipment, such as new pianos, chesterfields, magazine racks, and chess tables.[29] All of this outfitting, though, did not solve the problem, and in 1946 the executive temporarily closed the JCR, which led to three meetings over the competence of the executive to make that decision.[30] Various other steps were also taken, such as attempting to ban card playing and women from the room,[31] but none of these had any lasting effect.

The Lit. also styled itself as a political body throughout the 1930s, '40s, and '50s, claiming the right to represent all students at University College. This often resulted in conflict with the Students' Administrative Council (SAC), the central student body at the University of Toronto and the official representative of student opinion on campus. Any member of the Lit. had the right to propose a motion at an open meeting; if he could gain the assent of twenty of his fellow students, he could order the calling of a special open meeting to discuss his concerns. Two incidents from the early 1950s outline the conflicts this policy created. In October 1950 the Lit. passed a complex motion, the import of which was that the society would object to the removal of professors from the university because of communist leanings. The motion was passed 32 to 4, over the objections of SAC representative Bob Dnieper, who declared "The Lit. should confine itself to arguing about the costs of Follies sets and Arts Ball decorations ... and that it was useless for this society to take an interest in national and other affairs."[32] Dnieper then brought the motion to a SAC meeting, where it was tabled indefinitely, after Dnieper himself spoke against it. Dnieper was then censured by the Lit.[33]

The Russian Student Exchange was a more serious matter. A visit of Russian students to Canada had been proposed in 1950 and brought before the National Federation of Canadian University Students (NFCUS). NFCUS stalled on the issue, for fear that accepting the proposal would alienate the fiercely anti-communist Quebec universities and destroy the federation. The Lit. was less reticent, passing in November 1951 a motion 39 to 1 to approve the principle of Russian students visiting the Toronto campus.[34] NFCUS then went on to formally reject the exchange, which led to an emergency meeting of the Lit. to discuss the Russian visit. The Lit. unanimously passed a motion asking that SAC declare "that the University of Toronto severely censures the decision of the National Federation of Canadian University Students not to undertake the arrangement of a reciprocal visit between students of Canada and the USSR."[35] The Lit. briefly considered running its own exchange, but that idea did not make any headway.

WOMEN'S ORGANIZATIONS AND RELATIONS WITH THE LIT.

Women were first admitted to University College in 1884, but they were not allowed to become members of the all-male Lit. In the early years there were not enough women to warrant a separate organization, but in 1891 a meeting of "Lady Undergraduates of University College" was held. Attendees resolved to form a society "with the object of promoting literary work ... and encouraging public speaking."[36] The society's first meeting, held on 16 January 1892, showed the outlines of what the new organization, known as the Women's Literary Society, hoped to accomplish. The Glee Club sang, another student gave a solo, another a recitation, and then a debate occurred on the subject, "Resolved, That humanity has been more benefitted by Science than by Literature." Science won, and following the singing of a University College song and the national anthem the meeting was closed.[37]

The WLS, however, had to keep its meeting structure fluid, as it was always torn between "ornamental" activities, such as music and drama, and "practical" activities, such as debating and the reading of essays. Increasingly, songs, recitations, and dramatic presentations took up more of the WLS's time. One especially Tennyson-filled meeting prompted one critic to accuse the WLS of failing to promote "the strength and vivacity of intellect, the trained judgement, and the speedy grasp of problems which its founders regarded as essential to efficient work in any sphere of life."[38] The WLS responded that it was easier to persuade women students to participate in dramatic presentations than it was to get them to argue in debate, and "the first act would probably make the second seem easier."[39]

Change at the WLS was slow. In 1904 a year's activities included three debates, a play in either English or French, "lighter kinds of amusements in the shape of music or dramatic evenings," and the reading of papers.[40] From 1897 to 1901 the WLS published a journal, *Sesame*, and from 1898 on it had its own lending library, named after Grace Hall, a WLS member who had died in the summer of 1898.[41]

By 1909, however, the debate over the role of the university in public life had begun to affect the WLS. That year, the organization hosted speakers on Hull House in Chicago, and its parallel development, Evangelia Settlement in Toronto.[42] By 1911 it was organizing parliamentary-style debates, and in that year a bill for the establishment of a College for Women was defeated. In 1913 the WLS similarly debated and defeated a bill "that household science should be made a compulsory course for all pass women students in the Arts courses."[43]

At this point the WLS was in its last days as the central organization for women students at University College. A new administrative organization, known as the Women's Undergraduate Association (WUA), appeared in 1914, with one of its first goals being the development of a system "for regulating the number of offices that may be held by any one person" at the college.[44] Despite protests from supporters of the WLS, the WUA clearly supplanted the older organization, which existed into the 1930s. By 1917 the WUA had the support of a compulsory fee from all female students at University College, and it also administered an annual fee for the *Varsity*, the University of Toronto's main student newspaper.[45] Beyond administrative and financial details, the WUA took over the other concerns of women students that had been partially addressed by the WLS. For instance, in 1917 it dedicated two meetings to discussions of the use of federal franchise by university women,[46] and in 1919 it requested a gymnasium for women students.[47]

Between the two world wars, the WUA was more subdued. With the acquisition of a new Women's Union Building at 79 St George Street, the WUA gained its own space,[48] and it raised significant funds to furnish Whitney Hall residence, which was built in 1931.[49] What the WUA was to do in these new facilities was less clear. Although it asserted itself as the "self-government organization of the women of U.C.,"[50] the activities it ran did not live up to that image. Record-keeping was inordinately casual, and if minutes were taken they do not survive. The social events that the WUA hosted consisted entirely of an introductory meeting for incoming students and the occasional tea. The WUA's introductory meetings, which did not change in structure between 1923 and 1948, involved the president of the organization appealing to women students not to spend too much time on extracurricular activities, followed by representatives of clubs such as the Modern Languages Club and the Players' Guild inviting the students to support extracurricular pursuits to their fullest ability.[51]

Other WUA initiatives did occasionally surface. An annual prize in public speaking was presented after an "Oratorical Contest" in the 1920s, but it is unclear how long the tradition persisted.[52] In 1937 the WUA sponsored a lecture series entitled "The Modern Girl" and in 1939 another series on "Personality Hints."[53] After 1946 the anonymous donation of a trophy facilitated the WUA's desire to hold annual "Portia" debates in conjunction with the Lit.'s debates for the Robinette Shield.[54]

Apart from the issue of amalgamating with the Lit., the WUA's prime mission in the 1922 to 1959 period involved requiring all women at University College to wear academic gowns. This happened in two waves. The first was from 1923 to 1927, when the WUA sponsored an annual "Gown Week" under the assumption that once University College women put gowns on they would begin wearing them on a regular basis. Despite assurances given to the Varsity that the college gown was "heartily endorsed by all women students,"[55] by 1927 the president of the WUA was forced to admit that there had never been a successful Gown Week, and the idea did not survive the decade.[56]

The idea was revived in 1955, when the Varsity ran a headline entitled "WUA May Enforce Scarlet UC Gowns" and quoted the WUA president, Gay Sellers, who claimed that the idea was an undergraduate movement, not a top-down initiative.[57] Although a motion to approve the mandatory wearing of gowns was passed by a small majority at a sparsely attended meeting, the WUA could not make it stick. In January 1956 the WUA consequently declared that University College women were permitted, but not required, to wear gowns.[58]

Both the consumption of tea and the attempt to persuade women to wear gowns were clearly efforts by the WUA to preserve the dignity of campus women within a "separate sphere."[59] This concern was laudable, but seems to have convinced few women at the college. Despite the WUA's claims to be a representative body, it suffered from persistent crises of attendance that were far worse than the Lit. ever endured. Quorum at WUA meetings was sixty students; however, throughout the 1920s the WUA was hard pressed to get as many as fifty-five to show up, even to nominate candidates for elections.[60] In 1929 the association compromised by reducing the quorum requirement to thirty students, which solved the problem for the 1930s and 1940s. When the difficulty resurfaced in 1952, however, it was far worse. In January 1952 the executive of the WUA threatened to go on strike after only fifteen women attended a meeting,[61] and in 1954 the WUA was forced to dig people out of libraries and the JCR to obtain a bare quorum.[62] The WUA executive threatened to dissolve the organization, but was able to find enough students at one meeting (4 February 1954) to prevent that resolution from carrying.[63]

This recurring crisis of attendance at WUA meetings seems to have been directly connected to confusion over the organization's purpose. Attempts by the WUA to interest coeds in tea meetings and scarlet gowns ran contrary to the aims of most women at University College, who were pushing, step by step, towards formal amalgamation with the men and the completion of coeducation in student activities.

Signs of an active almagamation drive began to show in earnest in 1946, when the WUA attempted to change its name to the Women's Literary and Athletic Society, thus declaring that they considered them-selves an equivalent body to the men's society. The Lit. protested and the College Council ruled in its favour.[64] But the WUA was not easily held back, and it began to make the same sorts of political pronouncements as the Lit. In 1951, for example, the WUA backed the Russian Student Exchange,[65] and in 1952 it passed a motion to ask SAC "to investigate the firing of the six members of the Toronto Symphony Orchestra."[66]

The WUA's political interventions reflected the desire, held by many University College students, to foster joint activities between men and women. The thirty-year process of amalgamation began in 1921, when the Lit. challenged the WUA to a debate on equal pay for equal work.[67] In the 1930s the WUA and the Lit. met annually in at least one joint meeting, although there was always some confusion as to whether it was a cooperative activity or a concession by the Lit. to the "fairer sex."[68] The women resisted being treated as ornaments and defended their rights to control the agenda of the joint meetings, for example in 1935 when the women performed a well-orchestrated satire of the activ-ities of men at University College.[69] The joint meetings routinely drew more student attendees than any other activity of either organization, and also provided a prime opportunity for dancing.[70]

Through these meetings each group became more aware of the space controlled by the other. In 1938 the Lit. agreed to hold their Sunday concerts in the Women's Union. The next year the women of University College succeeded in becoming members of the Parliamen-tary Club, thereby joining the men to debate the issues of the day in the JCR, even if they were not permitted to sit for the group photo-graph.[71] By 1943 women were invited to the annual Soph-Frosh ban-quet, previously a men-only event, and in March 1944 the men and women voted simultaneously for their executives in the JCR.[72]

Amalgamation between the WUA and the Lit. was formally proposed in 1946[73] but was not consummated until thirteen years later. The many twists and turns of this saga are beyond the scope of the present book, but by the 1950s certain facts were clear. Neither the WUA nor the Lit.

could be assured that its meetings would gain a quorum, while joint activities did. The women of University College also had a large amount of money from fees and, unburdened by expenses such as the *Follies*, they could use this money to gain political clout. Evidence of this power appeared in 1955 when they WUA voted $1,000 to renovate the JCR under the condition that it become, formally, a coeducational space.[74] The WUA financial offensive continued the next year, when it passed a $3,529 budget and noted, pointedly, that $2,229 of this was going to joint activities with the men. The WUA then took the unprecedented step of holding an open meeting in the JCR, making real their claim that the space now belonged to both organizations.[75] This sort of display accelerated the process of amalgamation, which was finally approved in a joint meeting of one hundred students in the JCR on 23 January 1958.[76] The initial elections for the new organization, which continued to be known as the University College Literary and Athletic Society, drew record numbers of students.[77] With the union of the two bodies, the WUA and the idea of the "separate sphere" died at the student society level, although it held on for another decade in the residences of University College.

THE LIT. IN DECLINE

Unfortunately, the Lit.'s new structure was put into place just before the onset of the 1960s. That decade would highlight the differences between the organization of the Lit. and the spirit of the college it inhabited. A combination of aggressive individualism on the part of University College students and the new search for relevance at the university in general strained the Lit.'s ability to cope. Though the Lit. gained representation on University College Council, thus becoming an integral part of the administration of the college for the first time, the "old traditions" of the Canadian university system were on the verge of being submerged by a vast group of students who were creating a distinct youth culture based on action and change.[78]

Individualism was the initial insidious threat to the Lit., as continual reform movements sprang up to challenge the society's more frivolous expenditures, such as the purchase of athletic equipment and the subsidizing of dances. As Gary Perly put the matter in a debate in October 1963, "Why should we pay our student fees to subsidize clubs that we don't even belong to?"[79] Because students had ceased to attend Lit. meetings, the organization, after much discussion, abolished open meetings in 1965. At the same time the Lit. changed from having a ten-person executive that reported to an open meeting to being run by an eighteen-person council of representatives presided over by an executive of five. Thus ended a 111-year tradition.[80]

The issue of relevance was less immediately pressing, because the Lit. took a number of steps to place itself in the mainstream of student activist thought in the 1960s. These efforts began with "Current: Man in the Modern Age," a series of lectures and discussions presenting "questions relevant to the personal development of the undergraduate student," which featured such distinguished speakers as Emil Fackenheim, Northrop Frye, and Frank Underhill in its first year, and later such dignitaries as Eugene Rabinovitch and Arthur Schlesinger Jr.[81]

And then, in 1965, the Festival Era began at University College. From 1965 to 1968 the Lit. held several multi-day cultural festivals designed to capture "the vitality of modern life ... from a new ... culturally analytic perspective."[82] The "Pop Festival" in 1966 generated $1,500 in ticket sales, which allowed the Lit. to cover costs despite "two small fires" that broke out during the events.[83] In 1967, the popular "Perception '67" festival focussed on "the psychedelic experience" and, especially, the recreational and medicinal use of LSD.[84] Despite attempts by the Lit. to ensure a balanced approach to the discussions, this event was prohibited from being held at University College and had to be moved to Hart House.[85] Further difficulties ensued when festival organizers attempted to get Timothy Leary, on parole for transporting marijuana, to come to Canada to speak to the students. Though faculty supported the visit, the university stood by "dusty legalism" and refused to intervene to allow Leary to attend.[86] An attempt to meet Leary halfway in the Detroit/Windsor tunnel to acquire a tape of his comments was successful, but not without the student who was scheduled to drive Leary back to the United States being "bodily thrown into Canadian territory" and Leary himself being seized by Canadian immigration officials.[87] Despite these and other glitches, the 1967 festival was a success.

The same can not be said of "Propaganda '68: or Society as Madness and Myth," which suffered from cost over-runs, inexplicable displays, and the Mothers of Invention pouring shaving cream into the organ at Convocation Hall.[88] The Lit. also found itself threatened with several lawsuits. These, as well as the possibility of university censorship and further legal problems, led the Lit. to formally abandon plans for "Pornographia '69," thus ending the Festival Era.[89]

In addition to organizing counter-cultural festivals, the Lit. continued as a political body that engaged the issues of the 1960s. In so doing, the Lit. often came in to conflict with SAC, which in 1964 declared that it could make political decisions on social issues for the whole university campus.[90] The Lit. nonetheless clung to its independence, beginning in 1965 with the passing of a convoluted motion "authorizing the establishment of a committee to investigate the feasibility of setting up

a programme on the subject of birth control."[91] The Lit. also took
strong action on the Vietnam war, supporting draft-dodger organizations
in Toronto and, in 1969, voting $250 to help defray the legal expenses
of people arrested at an October 1968 anti-Vietnam War demonstration
in Toronto.[92]

In on-campus politics, by the end of the 1960s the Lit. finally gained
a voice on University College Council, the body that had the power
"to make rules and regulations for the government, direction, and
management" of the college.[93] Over the years the Council had often
stood in the way of the Lit. In 1965, for example, the Lit. attempted
to change its constitution to allow students who had failed their academic year to run for election to the organization; the Council, though,
upheld the primacy of academics over student politics.[94] The crisis over
"Perception '67" was the main catalyst of a resolution passed by the
Lit. in November 1967 calling for student representation on the Council. This desire for a voice existed despite statements by the principal
of the college, Douglas LePan, that the Council "did virtually nothing." In March 1968 the Council nonetheless approved student representation in principle, pending negotiations.[95] These negotiations were
prolonged, but by 1969 all outstanding issues were solved.[96]

The Lit.'s involvement in both off-campus and on-campus politics,
however, largely failed to impress the students of University College,
living as they were through an age of activism. As early as 1964 the
Lit. was having difficulty finding students to run for office. That year,
nine of eighteen seats, including the president and vice-president, were
filled by acclamation.[97] Participation rates at elections routinely
dropped close to, and then below, 10% of the college's population.[98]
By the beginning of the 1970s the problem had become critical. In
1970 the entire Lit. executive was acclaimed and, in 1971, an advertisement in the *Gargoyle* pitifully asked "WILL SOMEONE PLEASE
RUN."[99] This apathy led the Lit. into scandal in September 1972, when
it was without a treasurer because no student could be found to run
for the position the previous spring. The Lit. advertised the post as
vacant, and then welcomed a student named Lou Maag to the position
on an interim basis, pending Council approval. Maag, who was not a
student at University College or anywhere else, promptly took a
$10,000 cheque from the Comptroller of the University and attempted
to deposit it to his personal bank account. Fortunately, the banks had
been tipped off and the money was recovered.[100] The Lit., however,
had clearly reached rock bottom. It would not recover a prominent
position at University College for several years.

2 "Professional Gentlemen," 1854–90

ORIGINS AND DESTINATIONS

The traditional view of nineteenth-century University College students portrayed them all as unhewn products of Ontario farms, sent to university to be civilized. These impressions, which were stated as late as the 1950s,[1] are without quantitative substance. The image of University College as a humble collection of farmers' sons being trained to take roles in their local communities is not supported by my evidence, which points to quite different conclusions.

A significant proportion of the officers of the Literary and Scientific Society (28%) were born in or near Toronto. Outside of Toronto, southwestern Ontario was the other major location of origin, followed closely by eastern Ontario and the British Isles. Northern Ontario (which for the purposes of this study includes Ontario counties north and west of a line running through the middle of Perth County – roughly the line of greatest settlement before 1867) and the rest of Canada (not to say the world) did not provide a large number. Students came to the college because it was the closest one to home, a hypothesis supported by Gaffield, Marks, and Laskin's Queen's University study, which showed a similar percentage (61%) taking the shortest route to Kingston.[2] David Keane's data for 1879 entrants give a similar figure of 65% coming to University College from Toronto and points southwest.[3]

For this period, the number of fathers' occupations I have been able to identify is less than desired, especially given the fact that the names of most of the people are known. Missing early census records and cold trails in the British Isles are mostly responsible for the gaps. Even so, the data show that these Lit. officers were largely not farmers' sons. A quarter of them were children of professionals and a significant number were sons of businessmen and skilled workers. Even if all the unknown cases were considered to be farmers' children, they would still not be in a majority. Keane suggested that the figures for University College entrants on the whole would be between 29% and 40% farmers (he favoured 33%), with 24% belonging to the learned professions.[4] The data on birth location and parental occupation for the 319 officers of the Lit. are summarized in tables 2.1 and 2.2.

Thirty-three of the eighty-five professional fathers identified were clergymen, fifteen were politicians, eleven were lawyers or judges, ten were medical professionals, and nine were teachers (one at a university); seven others were scattered among architecture, engineering, journalism, and surveying. The businessmen were largely merchants and storekeepers, with a sizable number involved in lumber and the sawmill industry. Half of the skilled labourers were blacksmiths, carpenters, shoemakers, and tailors. At this distance it is difficult to reach any conclusions about the relative wealth of any of the parents. But it is clear that the students who ended up as officers of the Lit. in the early years came from diverse backgrounds.

Given the suppositions about University College in its early years, information about students' religious affiliations from this period (table 2.3) is equally interesting and, happily, more complete. The student population that emerges from the data hardly supports Bishop John Strachan's contention that this was a "godless" institution. Strachan called University College godless because the legislation that created it had removed the privileges the Anglican Church had secured at King's College. As William Westfall points out, however, University College kept many of the early staff of King's, who were ordained Anglican clergy, and these professors continued to teach natural and revealed religion under the thin disguise of "metaphysics and ethics."[5] Strachan's political defence of church and state cooperation in a provincial university, however, was no longer universally accepted. Even though Trinity College and Victoria College were close by, a large number of Anglicans and Methodists attended University College instead.

Keane suggests that the high percentage of Anglican students at University College was related "in part to the antagonism between high and low church elements in Ontario Anglicanism"; however, neither he nor I are able to answer decisively whether the University College Anglicans were "a measurably different group in their educational, social, or ethnic backgrounds from the Trinity College Anglicans"[6] or the other interesting questions about Methodists who avoided Victoria. Although a doctrinal gap among Anglicans would eventually lead to the formation of Wycliffe College (a Low Church institution), available information does not make it clear that the Anglicans who attended University College in these years shared such theological beliefs.

Not surprisingly, given the nature of the Lit.'s ideals and activities, and the aims and purpose of a university education, the nineteenth-century officers of the Lit. embarked on almost entirely professional careers. Among the "talking" professions for which the Lit. was supposed to provide training, the legal profession predominated. Tables 2.4 and 2.5 outline the occupational type and geographical location of the 319 subjects at ten and thirty years after graduation.

The former executives of the University College Lit. had a marked preference for living and working in Toronto. One figure stands out: fifty-eight Toronto lawyers, half the total number of lawyers, stayed in Toronto ten years after graduation. With the exception of Manitoba and British Columbia, in no other region did the number of lawyers outnumber the combined totals of the clergy, academic, and medically-trained graduates.

The history of the early days of the Literary and Scientific Society is the history of the Toronto Bar: this is the most striking conclusion that can be derived from the available data. One in three of the early officers of the Lit. became a lawyer, and half of those practised in Toronto. Even given the existence of significant courtroom activity, before 1900 the total number of lawyers in Toronto never reached more than 31% of all the lawyers in the province, so in this case the experience of the Lit. officers must be considered unusual.[7]

Does this popular career path completely explode the notion of students coming from and returning to the hinterland? The answer to this question is actually more complicated. A comparison of the birth and post-graduation geographical locations of the Lit. officers shows that 16% to 18% of all students born outside Toronto returned to the areas from which they originally came (for Toronto-born students the figure is slightly lower). Occupationally, this breaks down into approximately twenty lawyers, ten educationalists, five clergy, and four doctors. This pattern is consistent across all professions. The British-born did not significantly alter this data, either – only two of them returned to the areas where they received their early education. These figures must be taken, however, with several serious caveats. For approximately one-third of these early students, data on both birth and occupational locations are unavailable.

GENTLEMEN AT LAW

The next question concerns the relationship between university education and the professions to which these students gravitated. How did they fare in their chosen fields?

Historians of the legal profession in Ontario have remarked on more than one occasion that the practice of law in the nineteenth century did not require a university education. The most recent historian of the Law Society of Upper Canada states that in 1826 the Society began 150 years of "resistance to university-controlled legal education."[8] Gidney and Millar reiterate that theme in their comments that the Society had an uneasy relationship with legal education of a formal type, especially because it had little relevance to what lawyers actually did in the workplace.[9]

This tendency to denigrate formal university training, however, did not prevent prospective lawyers from attending university. Indeed, the university was one place where young men could receive the "liberal education rooted in the classics" that was "the mark of the gentleman" and necessary for passing the entrance examination to the bar.[10] Both Christopher Moore and Gidney and Millar point to the pressure among scholarly-minded law students to form associations that could offer some professional training. Moore especially notes the Osgoode Club, founded in 1847, which had a program of essays and debates designed to give young law students the edge they needed to succeed.[11]

The concept of a group of prospective lawyers getting together to partake of essay writing and debating as part of their training for professional gentlemanly life provided a rationale for a portion of the weekly activities of the University College Lit. While a university education provided a tangible benefit to prospective Law Society members in reducing by two the number of years after graduation required to qualify as barristers and attorneys,[12] it also offered an opportunity to make contacts and groom themselves for professional life. And these non-academic elements may have become more necessary as the nineteenth century progressed. Gidney and Millar note that both at mid-century and from the 1870s on the legal profession was a subject to attack by populist politicians.[13] The need for articulate defenders of professional rights must have seemed all the more necessary, and the Lit. was an excellent place to attain that ease of communication.

Apart from their professional benefits, legal training and a university education that included experience as an officer of the Lit. also proved to be channels to political involvement in later life. Of the 319 former Lit. officers during this first period, 55 (1 in 6) are known to have participated in political life by standing as candidates for office[14]; 41 of those were lawyers. And of the twenty-three who were members of provincial or dominion parliaments, all but three were lawyers at some point during their careers, the exceptions being Kitchener physician Dr Henry Lackner, Toronto cleric and educationalist Canon Henry Cody, and Dundas businessman Thomas Marshall.

Especially significant in this regard is the situation of the nine former Lit. officers who became lawyers in Manitoba. Of these, seven held political office – a percentage that is likely higher than that for university graduates as a whole in Manitoba. A few of these only held office for a short time as a prelude to being appointed judges in that province; but the fact remains that the combination of Lit. training, legal training, and the presence of mind to move west led to a great degree of political success. There was economic success to be had in the west as well. Arthur Wellington Ross used his professional credentials to collect fees on land transactions during Winnipeg's early boom-years, and both he and Heber Archibald were heavily involved in purchasing "child allotments" assigned to the Metis.[15]

This did not mean that those who stayed in Ontario were not successful in their profession. One of the more evident marks of success in the career of an Ontario lawyer was serving a term as a bencher of the Law Society of Upper Canada. No fewer than fourteen of the early Lit. officers took their seats in this body, either by appointment or (after 1871) by election among the lawyers of the province as a whole. These latter elections to the Law Society were themselves seemingly the direct effort of former officers of the Literary and Scientific Society.

The story of how Lit. training and camaraderie may have directly affected the Law Society's governance has escaped the attention of historians of Canadian law. They all note that Adam Crooks resigned as a bencher in 1866, saying that the lawyers in convocation had violated their principles by not appointing the candidate most worthy of the position, Edward Blake. Crooks declared "Blake's omission so outrageous that he could not remain in an appointive convocation."[16] Here the story gets somewhat murky, but by 1871 Ontario government legislation had made the benchers elective, and Crooks and Blake were duly elected to the position.

Lost in the story as told by the Law Society historians is the fact that both Crooks and Blake were ex-officers of the Lit., who had served together on the organization's first executives. The spirit of gentlemanly conduct engendered by the early Lit. appears to have led the two former student colleagues to transform the nature of the governing body of Ontario law. In the elections that followed in Ontario, Blake and Crooks were elected to the provincial legislature, along with Thomas Hodgins and Hammel De Roche, all lawyers, Liberals, and former Lit. executive members. Hodgins also become a bencher of the Law Society.

From their position in convocation, these former Lit. officers continued to look after their own. They saw, for instance, that George Eakins acceded to the control of the Law Library at Osgoode Hall.

Thomas Moss pressed for the re-opening of a law school in 1872, and that school had as lecturers Thomas Delamere and Thomas Hodgins.[17] And when the Osgoode Hall Law School was founded in 1889, they entrusted the office of first principal to William A. Reeve (who was introduced to his students by Edward Blake), and allowed John King and Samuel Bradford to teach there.[18] Having gained a sizable portion of the Toronto bar and having engineered their elections as benchers, the Lit.'s former officers moved forward to take control of Ontario's legal oligarchy.

This power was also secured by marriage alliances, taking advantage of what Christopher Moore calls "the continuing importance of family connections in the new era of professionalism."[19] Robert Baldwin, Robert Sullivan, Thomas Moss, William Glenholme Falconbridge, and Samuel H. Blake eventually all became members of the same extended family. Through marriage Edward Blake in turn came to be related to Charles McCaul, and further Blake family relations connected the Cronyns and Frederick Betts. In this way twenty lawyers and ex-officers of the Lit. could claim inter-relationship.

Similarly, Thomas Hodgins married a member of the Biggar family, and Charles Biggar in turn was related to Thomas Langton by virtue of their marriages to daughters of Oliver Mowat. Langton in turn was related to Ward Hamilton Bowlby. Another set of relations linked the Crombie brothers to William Durie Gwynne. Henry Coyne married one of the Bowes sisters and Malcolm Mercer and Herbert Irwin also ended up as relatives.[20] The sheer number of names points to the multiple connections that former Lit. officers forged through marital alliances as they entered into the legal profession.[21]

A study of their professional lives reveals further links among former Lit. officers. John A. Boyd was in partnership for seven years with the Blakes before ascending to the bench. Not only were Ernestus Crombie and William Gwynne related by marriage, they also shared a practice. Samuel Bradford and Malcolm Mercer also shared a practice of somewhat longer duration; it ended only when Mercer died in France in World War I. And when George Kennedy finally decided to enter the practice of law, he articled in the offices of Crooks and Cattanach, both of whom were his contemporaries on the Lit.

My identification of these personal and professional relationships is the result of a cursory scan of available data, and yet already over half of the ex-officers of the Lit. who became lawyers can be found connected to one another. They all shared a common educational background, had all argued with each other and ran with and against each other in elections, and in the process had forged a common set of values that led them to perform as a mutual support and admiration society for the remainder of their lives.

There were, of course, other ways to attain prominence in the legal profession in Ontario without being connected to the Literary and Scientific Society of University College. W.A. Reeve, to cite one example, not only had friends among the benchers from his college days but could also count among them two benchers, Stephen Richards and Byron Britton, with whom he had articled and for whom the Lit. meant nothing at all. And Reeve's replacement as principal of Osgoode Hall Law School, Newman W. Hoyles, had no connection to University College.[22] In an era that lacked common educational training for young lawyers, however, the early connections mentioned above must be recognized, especially because they are absent in later periods.

In the fullness of time, sixteen former Lit. officers were named judges. Half of those were not in Ontario, with three in Manitoba, two in British Columbia, and one each in Michigan and Illinois. Lyman Duff became chief justice of the Supreme Court of Canada and merited a full-length biography of his life in Canadian law.[23]

With every success remembered, however, comes a ne'er-do-well forgotten. Not all lawyers that the Lit. executive produced were able to exploit patronage and marriage in order to make their lives a success. Daniel Henry Mooney tried for years to obtain a suitable appointment, finally ending up as the bursar of the Toronto Lunatic Asylum, where too-close proximity to the inmates drove him to suicide because he feared his brain was "softening" in the job.[24] Arthur Freeman Lobb attempted to combine his legal practice with real estate, landed himself in financial trouble, and had to flee Toronto and eventually the country as a result, dying discredited and nearly forgotten on a farm in Minnesota. William Creelman gave up a promising role with the Blake firm and died of dysentery in the Philippines during the Spanish-American War. And Dugald MacMurchy shot his leg off in a hunting accident and died of gangrene. These cases, among the dozen or so that could be mentioned, show that the combination of the Lit. and the law was not foolproof.

GENTLEMEN AT CHURCH

It is not surprising that ex-officers of the Lit. in this period were found among the clergy. This profession was one of the few in late-nineteenth-century Canada that gave preference to university-level training.[25] Although in the early part of the century clergy could be trained by apprenticeship, by the 1840s all denominations were creating institutions to replace this system, even if some older clerics fought the process.[26] As well, to be a clergyman in Canada, and especially in Ontario, was to be part of an important segment of society. The Sunday sermon was a popular entertainment in most places in the province, and those with oratorical pretensions could find the pulpit an excellent place to exhibit their skills.[27]

However, Gidney and Millar also point out contrary trends in the clergy as a profession during the nineteenth century. Surplus clerics kept wages down, causing some to leave the ministry entirely. By the latter part of the century the rise of voluntarism in Ontario and the notion of ministers as employees of a congregation rather than part of the apparatus of an established state church caused a crisis of confidence among clergymen as to their place in society.[28] These trends had their effect, it seems, on the career choices of Lit. officers. While over one hundred ended up in law, forty-nine spent significant time as ministers.

The first surprising point about these forty-nine is that they span all the denominations in Ontario at the time. They include twenty-nine Presbyterians, ten Anglicans, four Methodists, two Baptists, two Roman Catholics, one Christian Scientist, and one Unitarian. Despite those like Bishop Strachan who derided it as godless, University College still managed to have its presence felt as a place of first education for those heading into the Methodist and Anglican ministries, even though Victoria College and Trinity College were better suited for the purpose.

The connection between University College and the training of Anglican clergy emerged from church politics in the Diocese of Toronto in the 1860s. Certain churchmen, distressed about an increase in clerical ritualism in the diocese, formed the Church of England Evangelical Association to defend their rights to have religious practice more in keeping with the spirit of the Protestant Reformation.[29] These churchmen formed several support organizations, including a new training facility for an Evangelical Anglican clergy that became known as Wycliffe College.[30] Among the earliest supporters of this institution was Professor Daniel Wilson of University College, and it was in fact from University College that Wycliffe received many of its early students.[31] Wycliffe also formally affiliated with the University of Toronto and used University College as the site for preliminary arts training for its students.[32]

With the exception of Stuart Foster, who quit the priesthood to teach and died young, all the other Lit. officers who entered the Anglican clergy reached a degree of prominence, three becoming archdeacons and one a bishop. Four of them had to do so, however, outside of Canada, most likely because their connection with Wycliffe College made it impossible for them to receive ordination from the bishop of Toronto. Edward Acheson, the one bishop, held his position in Japan.

The record of success for Anglican clergymen who were also ex-officers of the Lit. is a testimony to the oratorical training and political skills that the society provided.

Presbyterians had been using University College as an educational support for the training of their clergy since the beginning of the institution. Although Knox College, founded in 1844, had always possessed its own preparatory department for instruction in arts courses, many of the courses in Knox's three-year, non-theological program were taught at University College.[33] After 1881, Knox required an arts degree from an approved university as a prerequisite for its Bachelor of Divinity degree.[34] Knox completed the process of identification with University College by formally affiliating itself with the University of Toronto in 1885.[35]

The leadership record of those ex-officers of the Lit. who became Presbyterian clergy was somewhat mixed. Four were elected as moderators of the church in Canada, and one in England – a respectable success rate. More important, however, was the support in other areas that Presbyterian ministers who were former Lit. officers provided.

Five of these men became professors. George Bryce went to Manitoba College in Winnipeg and "wielded a great influence and made a lasting name" during his years there.[36] The others became prominent scholars and mainstays at the Presbyterian College in Montreal and Knox College.[37] Not content to merely be clergy, these men dedicated their lives to reproducing church leaders in their image by actively taking a role in the theological colleges whose influences were supposed to be critical in the "process of clerical foundation."[38] Other ordained clergy attempted to do the same for the Anglicans at Wycliffe and St. John's College in Winnipeg, the Baptists at McMaster University, and the Catholics at St. Michael's College. Presbyterian ministers were also active outside the realm of theology at other educational institutions. John MacMillan taught sociology at Victoria College, and Angus McLeod became the first principal of the Regina Industrial School, the main purpose of which was "to transmit to the native students an appreciation of Christianity while preparing them to adapt and conform to the Canadian way of life by learning English and mastering a trade."[39]

Four Presbyterians also became prominent in the sphere of church publication. Robert Haddow and Robert D. Fraser, for example, succeeded each other as editor of the *Presbyterian Witness*. William McKenzie performed a similar role for the Christian Scientists in Massachusetts and gained an entry in *Who's Who in America* for his troubles.

Two further Presbyterians were active in the Home Missions movement, spreading the church's influence far beyond the walls of University

College. These men represent two-thirds of the missionaries produced by this generation of Lit. officers, the only other one being John Craig, who spent nearly his entire life working for the Baptists in India.

The eighteen clergy/professors, clergy/editors, and clergy/missionaries constituted one serious response to the problems of overcrowding in the Christian churches during the nineteenth century. With the life of a minister being fraught with uncertainty, these men declined to restrict their activities to that one role. Four others reacted by leaving the ministry entirely to teach. And John H. Long was even more innovative, combining his Unitarian ministry with an active legal practice. As a group, the Lit. executive members who entered the clergy actively engaged the crisis in their profession and found niches that could sustain them.

In terms of their religious philosophies, no clear picture emerges. The Lit. does not seem to have forged a consensus about the proper role of religion in society, which may not be surprising given that discussion of religious topics was not permitted there. A conservative streak can, though, be noted among some. John Campbell and John Scrimger (Presbyterians) and Francis Wallace (Methodist) are among those whom Michael Gauvreau has identified as exercising the utmost caution in reconciling historical criticism and evangelical Christianity in order to avoid radical change.[40] Politically, W.T. Herridge was among the few in the Presbyterian Church unwilling to enthusiastically embrace labour during the 1919 Winnipeg crisis, and Henry John Cody proved himself a moderate on issues of Prohibition and Canadian activist foreign policy, and at one point was a cabinet minister in a Conservative government in Ontario.[41]

But then there are the counter cases. The most notable of these is Nelson Burns, who broke with the Methodists and founded his own "holiness" movement, which confounded moderates and led to his eviction from the Methodist Church in 1894.[42] William G.W. Fortune, meanwhile, became a leader of the temperance movements in Alberta and British Columbia. And at least five of the Presbyterians were active crusaders for the United Church movement, three living to join that new body.

Still, the Lit.'s impact on the clergy of Canada appears to have been limited. As a vehicle for personal development it was certainly useful. It may also have instilled a love of education that carried over into career choices. But in the end, by forbidding the discussion of theology at its meetings, the society, in contrast to its impact on the law, did not generate a "Lit. style" of acting in the profession. As William Westfall aptly puts it, "the formation of clergy ... proved to be part of a lifelong process in which a large number of factors played a crucial role ... The process of clerical formation was by no means restricted to what went on within the walls of a seminary or college."[43]

GENTLEMEN IN THE CLASSROOM

The ex-officers of the Lit. were all, by the end of their student lives, possessors of some educational attainment. They also, through their experiences with the organization, had developed a skill at public speaking. The combination of the two attributes was good preparation for a career in the teaching profession, and 67 of the 319 in this period became teachers.

For twenty-two of them, teaching was not enough. Their experience in a university environment had proved to be so pleasing that they declined to leave it and became university professors. Thirteen of these, indeed, stayed on to become professors at the University of Toronto, one (William Dale) even having to suffer the pain of being fired by his alma mater. Seven made their professional careers in the United States, and the remaining two ended up at Royal Military College and Queen's University. Ex-officers of the Lit. who became professors made almost no attempt to spread themselves among Canadian universities the way the clergy spread themselves among denominations; for most of this generation it was their alma mater or another country. The nepotistic way in which university appointments were made before the reform of this process at the University of Toronto in 1906 no doubt made this habit of staying put much easier.

For those who emigrated to the United States, several made careers significant enough to merit inclusion in *Who's Who in America*. Lewellys F. Barker and Wilfred Mustard became prominent at Johns Hopkins University and Henry Fairclough gained a reputation as a professor of classics at Stanford.[44]

The small number of cases, though, makes it impossible to claim that the Lit. was a training ground for superior academics. It is more likely that talented students tended to be selected by the University College electorate to serve in office, and that these people consequently became good professors. The political skills developed through involvement in the Lit. did not, however, transfer especially well to the academic political process and allow these scholars to advance to high administrative ranks at their universities. It is true that two presidents of the University of Toronto (James Loudon and Henry Cody) did have Lit. experience, but Cody managed to gain the post without ever holding a position as a professor. It is hard to make a case that these two, as well as Frederick Sykes of the Connecticut College for Women, reached these ranks because of the Lit.

For those who stayed in lower branches of education, the case for academic leadership may be somewhat better. Forty-five of the teachers in the sample taught at the high school level.[45] Gidney and Millar point out that the claim of school teachers in Ontario to professional status in the nineteenth century was tenuous, because the learned status of the profession was balanced by the high percentage of female teachers and the notion that teachers were employees of the state.[46] However, they concede that this problem was more serious for elementary school teachers, and that high school instructors were better off, "substantially better paid," and referred to in educational reports as gentlemen and ladies.[47] Certainly, the ex-officers of the Lit. were well aware of this distinction, as not one made a career in the elementary school system – a gentleman taught high school.

Even the status of high school teacher was often not enough. Twenty-five, or 55%, became principals and headmasters, on the whole not in backwater towns. Five ended up in Toronto, four in Hamilton, two in Ottawa, and others worked in significant urban areas. Some of the principals in lesser towns ascended to their positions at young ages and then either died or left the profession. Those who survived and remained teaching gravitated to larger centres in the province and, almost entirely, to the collegiate institutes or private schools, where they would attempt to guide the next generation of an educational elite.

Not all the high school teachers, of course, stayed in their original profession. Eight decided that teaching was not profitable, prominent, or fulfilling enough for their liking. Six of these quit to enter the law, and two to become businessmen. The most successful of these men who made occupational changes was most likely Hammel De Roche, who resigned as principal of Napanee High School, became a lawyer, and then served twelve years as a member of the provincial parliament. For those with such professional and political aspirations, the high schools were an insufficient launching pad.

Given the critical mass of ex-Lit. officers at the University of Toronto and in the surrounding high schools, the possibility of networking in order to secure high-quality students for their alma mater could have occurred. As Gidney and Millar note in their history of the foundation of secondary school education in Ontario, "the high schools were now vital reservoirs of students that the universities needed to tap."[48] Any means by which the University of Toronto could be promoted at the high school level would keep the flow of students coming. In 1884, Edward Blake addressed convocation at the university and referred to the "close practical relation between the University and those institutions of high training which are known as Collegiate Institutes and

High Schools throughout the province," going on to note that the University of Toronto had graduated fifty-one of the ninety-four head-masters of these institutions.[49] The *Varsity* published a historical chart documenting this rise, summarized in table 2.6.

The ex-officers of the Lit. in this period were joining a group that was dominating Ontario's educational hierarchy. It is not known to what extent the University was able to use its success rate in the education field as a means to improve the later fortunes of the institution. What is clear is that those students who were involved with the Lit. in subsequent years had a group of successful men to invoke as justification for the continuation of their organization in the face of student apathy and criticism.

GENTLEMEN IN OTHER PROFESSIONS

I have identified forty-one of the ex-officers of the Lit. as having entered professions other than the primary talking careers in the law, clergy, and education. The limited spread of their careers shows how narrow the vista was for nineteenth-century university graduates.

Twenty former officers became physicians. This number may be smaller than expected, though it should be noted that while the medical profession expanded substantially in Ontario during the nineteeth century, few doctors obtained arts degrees. The reason for the limited number is connected to the nature of the Literary and Scientific Society itself. The Lit. was an organization for students in arts and sciences. Very few medical students chose this route to their degrees, as medical and arts education at the University of Toronto were essentially separate tracks that rarely crossed. Most of the doctors who had experience with the Lit. were the ex-officio representatives of the medical students at a time when the Lit. had dreams of being the representative institution for the whole university. Few of them were noted for their participation at meetings; they merely legitimized the annual struggle to get medical students to cast their votes at Lit. elections. Three medical graduates eventually became professors, and the other seventeen spread around the world. One (Alexander Crichton) was thrown out of the profession for his persistent support of patent medicine sales; the others adhered to their careers for their entire lives.

Ten other graduates pursued lives in business. Three of these did so in the United States, perhaps the most prominent being Nicholas Monsarrat, who became president of several Ohio railway concerns. Of the seven who stayed in Canada, four took over businesses started by their parents. Only one of these ten (John C. Stuart) failed to own his own business and became an employee at someone else's lumber company in Windsor. Businessmen were not considered "professional gentlemen" in this period, but at least most of them could claim the independence of action that the term connoted.

A further seven went into journalism, as writers, editors, and authors. Two of these eventually quit their jobs to become businessmen, and another (James Ross) joined the Red River Rebellion and died for his pains. Nineteenth-century journalism did not enjoy the respect of the learned professions, and those seven who turned their backs on their training to stain their hands with ink most likely would have suffered the contempt expressed by William Loudon:

The President of the Literary Society for 1859–60 was William Jordan Rattray, one of the most promising students of the early 'sixties ... Rattray had sterling qualities of mind which his competitors never possessed. Unfortunately, while others of his time took leading parts in the history of their country, he became, through circumstances which were all of his own making, a derelict, and spent his short life in writing newspaper articles and editorials. The only thing he had left behind him for future generations is his history in four volumes entitled *The Scot in British North America*.[50]

While Rattray achieved posthumous fame in the *Dictionary of Canadian Biography*, during the nineteenth century writing four-volume histories of Scots was not considered the proper task for student leaders.

That list leaves four rogue cases among the forty-one I have identified. Three of them can be considered to have belonged to professions in the making: accounting, engineering, and the civil service. More will be said about these career choices in later sections, but they were available, if a bit odd and surprising, for university graduates to consider in the nineteenth century.

The last student, Joseph Burr Tyrrell, became a renowned explorer and geographer of the Canadian North before quitting to become a mining engineer in the Yukon and then, in his later years, a consulting engineer in Toronto. He travelled perhaps more miles than any ex-officer of the Lit. from this period, and his career truly ranks among the strangest of the staid lawyers, clerics, and high school principals discussed above. But Tyrrell was, at base, no different from his peers. He attended law school and had desires to continue on in the legal profession. The only thing that prevented Tyrrell was the advice of his doctors, who warned him that practising law would be injurious to his health and advised an outdoor career. Unlike other young lawyers from this group who worked themselves to an early death, Tyrrell took this advice and made the most of what an outdoor career could provide in this period of Canadian history. He, too, received a full-length biography and was seen as a model for others to follow for future historians of the Lit.[51] If "professional geographer" was an unknown category in the thinking of those who debated at University College in the 1860s,[52] it would not be to the generations who came after.

CHARACTER AND CAREER

From 1854 to 1890 the Literary and Scientific Society of University College was an institution dedicated to the propagation of oratorical skills and gentlemanly values. Although the degree to which the Lit. succeeded in inculcating these skills and values was unclear to its critics, the results were evident in the choices of careers to which former officers eventually proceeded.

Recent scholarship has pointed out the connection between university training, gentlemanly conduct, and professional careers. Those who participated in the activities of the Lit. were probably not, however, as materialistic as this argument makes them seem. As Burton Bledstein points out, mid-Victorian Americans were just as interested in "character" as in "career," and the idea of character was shifting to include formation "by aggressive mental initiative, self-reliance, and usefulness." At University College these credentials could be cultivated through participation in the Lit., and certainly officers of the Lit. would have spoken to the character of their members if they were asked. In the case of the United States, however, Bledstein notes that beginning in 1870 the universities became "a vital part in the culture of professionalism ... the testing ground for the kind of world an energetic middle class sought to create for itself."[53] Canadian universities in time became similar institutions, but for the purposes of this chapter the lines between "character training" and "professional training" have been blurred. They were two names for the same thing, as far as the learned professions were concerned.

And nearly all the former officers of the Lit. took their places in the learned professions. In those roles some of them rose to positions of high rank and influence that can be measured and described, such as Allen Aylesworth, Lyman Duff, and Henry Cody. Others ended up in places and occupations in which their relative influence cannot be determined, and some were outright failures, like Daniel Mooney and James Ross. In the nineteenth century the Lit., in and of itself, was no sure route to occupational success for students with professional aspirations.

In the law and in the high schools, however, Lit. experience noticeably affected future success. A higher percentage of ex-officers in both these fields reached positions of influence than the general rate for that profession. In the law, this was partly because of efficient and flagrant use of kinship networks and previous connections to control Convocation of the Law Society and the newly emerging law school. In the world of high school education, the means by which success was effected are less clear; however, it is certain that Lit. connections could be and were used. The rising fortunes of former officers provided a list of individual successes to which the Lit. could point in future years as it dealt with the new issues and crises that arose after the Great Fire of 1890.

3 Political Animals:
The University College Lit.,
1891–1921

ORIGINS AND DESTINATIONS

There is no accepted set of assumptions about the social origins of male Canadian university students between 1891 and 1921. There are also no comments from contemporary observers or later scholars that can be used to test the typicality of the officers of the University College Literary and Scientific Society.[1] Studies of student life in this period concentrate on what students did, not on who they were. However, it is possible to trace changes in the Lit. student body from 1891 to 1921 by comparing it to the earlier cohort.

The birthplaces of the Lit. officers for this period differ somewhat from the earlier period. The number of British-born had declined substantially, and with it the total of non-Canadians attending University College. In addition, fewer students from the rest of Canada were enrolled. There is no doubt that this change occurred because of the opening of universities in other provinces. The University of Toronto no longer was the only post-secondary institution available for western Canadians, and it increasingly served as a training ground primarily for students from Ontario. In the Ontario data, the only figure to change substantially was for northern Ontario, not surprisingly as the settlement line in the province moved steadily further north. For this period, unlike the previous one, we are dealing with a provincial and not a national institution (see table 3.1).

In terms of parental occupation (table 3.2), the changes were slight but revealing. Professionals were sending slightly fewer of their sons to University College, while businessmen were sending more. Fewer skilled labourers and more white collar workers were the fathers of this cohort of students. Canadian occupational data as listed in the census showed that some of this shift was consistent with changing trends in general society. Between 1901 and 1921, for example, the percentage of Canadians in business and white-collar occupations increased at the expense of the traditional professions.[2] Beyond the growth in numbers of these groups, there was also a growing understanding that a university education could have connections to industrial and business expansion. Some of the fathers who sent their sons to university were likely among those pressing for changes in higher education, such as more focus on technology and "practical science."[3] Paul Axelrod has pointed out that "universities found that their own prestige could be enhanced by establishing their relevance to an expanding industrial society."[4] Businessmen were discovering the value of university education, and universities were realizing the benefits of making education more palatable to their ideas about how their sons should be trained.

Among the professional fathers, the most striking decline was among the clergy. Only nineteen Lit. officers' fathers were clergymen. This decline from 10% to 4% may have resulted from the falling income various denominations experienced during this period, and that made it more difficult for clergy to send their children to university. Another explanation might be that academic staff increasingly did not have to be ordained; during the period the number of fathers who were academics rose to twenty-four (i.e., from 2% to 6%), if one includes four school inspectors. The number of medical men also increased to twenty-six, including four dentists (a rise from 3% to 6%), while the number of lawyers rose to twenty-one (an increase from 3% to 6%). Four fathers were politicians and eleven other professionals accounted for 3% of the total, down from 5% in the last period. As these tallies show, the fathers of the 1891–1921 Lit. officers who were professionals were concentrated in law, medicine, and education.

The businessmen fathers, meanwhile, were more mixed. Forty of them were merchants and storekeepers, but there were also ten manufacturers, five hotel-keepers, and five in life insurance. The insurance business debuted as a new parental occupation in this period, and it speaks to the growth of Canadian financial institutions, something also shown by the presence of two bankers among the fathers. Moving further down the occupational hierarchy, the presence of ten civil servants indicates the new respect accorded to, and increased remuneration received by, government employees.

In terms of Lit. officers' religious affiliations (table 3.3), the Anglicans dropped from 34% to 22% in this later period. Presbyterians rose from 41% to 47%, and Methodists jumped slightly from 14% to 16%. Roman Catholics also increased (1% to 6%) while Baptists held almost steady (5% to 4%). It is difficult to make much of these data at first sight, because there was also a significant drop in the percentage of cases in which religion is unknown, and these may have turned out all to be Presbyterians. Even in this later period, significant Anglican, Methodist, and Roman Catholic populations were attending University College for an arts education. Considering that after 1891 Victoria College was located in Toronto and federated with the University of Toronto, and that Trinity College joined the university in 1903, the enrolment of so many Methodists and Anglicans is somewhat strange. It most likely reflected either doctrinal differences among denominations, personal/parental preference for a state institution over a religious college, or the fact that Queen Street West, where Trinity was located until 1925, was beyond the pale for many Toronto residents.

Tables 3.4 and 3.5 show the occupational and geographical paths of the Lit. officers for this period. They still overwhelmingly became professionals, but increasing numbers also went into business, and many more entered occupations as managers and white-collar workers, at least in the early years after graduation.[5] White-collar percentages did drop significantly as the group aged, but for their early years at least these students were employees and not independent professionals. To some extent the figures for supervisory and artisan-skilled occupational groups were inflated by the experience of World War I, as "infantry officer" and "soldier" became the occupations of many of the Lit. executives shortly after graduation.[6]

The changing patterns of student career decisions can be sketched using the occupational breakdowns ten years after graduation (table 3.6). The preponderance of Lit. members choosing to enter the legal profession during this period declined significantly. If one counts the scientists as belonging to the "academic" category, this figure was reasonably steady. The number of doctors, however, rose, and journalists doubled in number as an occupational category. New in this period was the emergence of the professional engineer, partly because of cooperation between the School of Practical Science (SPS) and the Lit., to which two engineering representatives a year were elected. These engineers, however, would not have been around at all had there not been an increase in university training available in their field.[7]

It is worth considering to what extent the occupational choice of this cohort of Lit. officers was already determined before they became involved in the society. From 1904 on, the application forms for registration at the University of Toronto included a question on intended occupation after graduation. In some cases this was left blank, but for the period 1904 to 1921 seventy-six future Lit. officers stated their intended occupations. The data (recorded in table 3.7) show the limited range of intended post-university employment in the period, and also that many more students imagined pursuing legal and academic careers than actually followed through. One can add to the list of officers who achieved their stated occupational objectives the twelve lawyers, one clergyman, two doctors, seven academics, three journalists, ten businessmen, one civil servant, two farmers, and one political organizer who embarked on the same careers as their fathers had. This brings to eighty-five the total of known cases in which a student's occupational dreams were formulated either during his home life or at some other point before attending University College.

The decline in numbers entering the legal profession was similar to the career situation in the province of Ontario as a whole. From 1901 to 1911 especially, the number of lawyers in the province dropped from 1,770 to 1,638, and from 1911 to 1921 the number rose only to 1,899. Relative to the general population, Ontario lawyers consistently declined in number during the time when this group of Lit. officers were making their career decisions.[8] While Curtis Cole attributes this decline to the unsettled nature of the legal profession, Christopher Moore notes that within five years of the opening of the Osgoode Hall Law School in 1889, bar calls in Ontario were falling steadily. Moore also notes, however, that the number of students who held university degrees upon entering legal studies was rising, so it does not seem that Osgoode Hall was to blame for the drop in university numbers.[9]

As a result of the First World War the destinations of former Lit. officers (and many other patriotic Canadians) for much of this period were determined by the needs of the Canadian armed forces. For ten years after graduation the figures for overseas occupations are higher than normal and cannot be considered for comparative purposes. The peacetime figures on location thirty years after graduation are more reliable. Over one-third (36%) of the cohort were in Toronto, 60% in Ontario counting Toronto, 83% in Canada counting Ontario, 13% in the United States, and 4% overseas. Comparing these data with the first period, residence in Toronto had declined (50% vs. 36%) as it had in Ontario (74% vs. 60%) and in Canada (87% vs. 83%).

Occupational differences are also revealing. Lawyers in Toronto no longer dominated. The new legal frontier had moved from Manitoba to Alberta (which was made a province in 1905), but not to Saskatchewan. The academics stayed in Toronto or went to the United

States, except for a new and growing percentage destined for Western Canada as its educational facilities continued to develop around the turn of the century. The clergy were still spread widely, but a significant number settled in Toronto.

In Toronto as well, much more occupational diversity was evident, as more students sought other careers there. The breakdown for all occupations in Toronto twenty years after graduation is shown in table 3.8. Especially notable is the increase in managers among the Toronto group. They included a general manager at Ontario Hydro, a manager at the Liquor Control Board of Ontario, a public relations manager for Simpson's department store, and a manager of a movie company. As Toronto grew as an urban centre, the need for intelligent management grew as well, and ex-officers of the Lit. were able to supply part of this need. The seven managers in Toronto represented 70% of the ten former officers of the Lit. who were managing things twenty years after graduation.

The number who received the designation civil servant is only three. But when managers of government agencies, government-employed scientists, school superintendents, a "Dominion Archivist," and the like are included, the number rises significantly to twenty-six, including three lawyers who acted primarily as legal counsel for municipal, provincial, and federal governments. This raises the percentage of civil servants, generously defined, from 1% to 7%. High school teachers, if included, would increase the proportion even more, but for this period they were not generally considered members of the civil service.

POLITICAL ANIMALS

Surely, political animals should be found in politics. The Literary and Scientific Society was obsessed with political activity and in the latter part of the 1891–1921 period made an overt attempt to move to party politics at a university level. This was in direct response to pressure from elders who wished to see more participation in public life by university graduates and who believed the Lit. was the proper training ground for this.

Political participation by former Lit. officers, however, *dropped* during this period. While 17% of the 1854–90 cohort eventually made a run for political office, in the 1891–1921 period the number of political hopefuls fell to 12% (45 of 379). The figure of twenty-three members of dominion and provincial parliaments in 1854–90 plummets to eleven for 1891–1921. Looking at these statistics, it is not improbable that the noble period of political experiment by the University College Lit. had no effect at all. In fact, only seven of the forty-five political contenders were students during the straight political period from 1912 to 1915, and not one sat in federal parliament until 1955, when Thomas D'Arcy Leonard was appointed to the Senate of Canada.

The idea of the Lit. as a political training ground, though, had great durability. Looking back on this period in 1934, the *Varsity* recalled that "politics and political parties were prevalent. Elections became mere excuses for street brawls. At the same time, however, there were some excellent debates, with men of such calibre as Rt. Hon. Arthur Meighn [*sic*], G. Howard Ferguson, George S. Henry, and Mackenzie King debating."[10]

These names were not selected accidentally, and they are four cases that bear exploring in order to understand the role of the Lit. in postgraduate political life. William Lyon Mackenzie King, Arthur Meighen, George Stuart Henry, and George Howard Ferguson all attended University College in the 1891–95 period. All four rose to the top of the Canadian political ladder. To what extent can the Lit. be considered responsible for their successes?

R. MacGregor Dawson reported in 1958 that King "appeared in debates before the Literary Society and was in some demand as an after-dinner speaker. But on the whole these occasions were infrequent."[11] Dawson placed far more emphasis on King's participation in the student strike of 1895. The minutes of the Lit. may not have been available to Dawson, but they show that King took part in four debates while a member. His side won every debate he participated in: "whether the French Revolution was more justifiable than the American Revolution" (affirmative), whether prohibition of alcohol was useful (negative), that the direct election of county officials by the county electors would be in the best interests of the county (negative), and that the War of Independence did more to advance the United States than the Civil War (affirmative).[12] Election as a speaker at a public debate was a selectively accorded honour, and it speaks to the opinion that King's fellow students held of him in 1894.[13] Of course, his role in 1895 remains controversial. Ian Montagnes in 1955 asked:

Meanwhile, what of young Mackenzie King? History has always considered him a hero of the movement. Certainly he was one of the students elected at the end of the strike to discuss grievances with the University Council. Yet, according to A.M. Chisholm, another strike leader, King was far from a hero ... Chisholm recalls King as the only member of the graduating class who attended lectures during the strike. For this, he says, King was ostracized as a double-crosser after his stirring speech at the protest meeting ... King, however, was happy to maintain in later life the story of his strike role.[14]

Even if his role was less than stellar, up until the strike King had been an active participant in the affairs of the Lit.

The case for Arthur Meighen is somewhat weaker. Roger Graham in 1960 attested that Meighen had enjoyed a quiet university career: "Such diversion as he allowed himself he found in the meetings of the Literary and Scientific Society ... Meighen was a sporadic attendant at the weekly meetings of the 'Lit' and took part in two of its debates" as well as participated in two mock parliaments.[15] At least one of the debates was given much significance by R.A. Bell in his history of the Lit. "The Man who conducted the Bill to establish the Canadian National Railways through the House of Commons must have remembered the debate on November 12, 1895, 'resolved that the government should have full control of railways.'"[16] Meighen lost both debates, in contrast to King's successes. Meighen also withdrew from the same election for public debater that King won in 1894, most likely because he saw no need to participate and considered the nomination honour enough.[17] One honour he did not decline was the opportunity to audit the treasurer's reports in March 1895. This nomination shows that the Lit. respected his mathematical abilities.[18] Graham, however, does not want to link this period directly with Meighen's decision to enter politics. He does, though, speak of the "highly developed political consciousness of his home and community" that had "been ingrained in him" and "was strengthened as he grew up."[19] Certainly the University College Literary and Scientific Society must be reckoned as part of this growing-up process.

Unfortunately, no biographical commentator can be cited on the subject of George S. Henry's university activities. The only evidence of them that remains is found in his personal papers at the Public Archives of Ontario (PAO). Henry paid such deep attention to the Lit. election of 1895 that he preserved, intact, four election posters printed by the two parties involved.[20] This speaks to an interest in electioneering that may have pointed to a future political career, but of the four his case is the weakest.

That leaves George Howard Ferguson, who eventually served as premier of Ontario for eight years (1923–30). In Ferguson's case there is a biography, but one that skips too lightly over his student days. Ferguson was the only one of these four to be elected to office with the Lit., but there is more to the Ferguson story than that. Exactly what this is can be shown by a partial report of Nomination Night at the Literary and Scientific Society, March 1891:

The excitement was becoming more and more intense, when the voice of the President was heard asking for nominations for the office of First Vice-President.

There was a commotion in the ranks of the Federals, a long pent up cheer broke forth and Mr. G.H. Ferguson was hoisted on to the platform by his enthusiastic followers ... At last the oracle spoke, "I wish to submit to the meeting the name of a gentleman of *sound judgement and calm deliberation.*" And then what a howl went up to heaven through the skylights! ... The voice of the speaker re-iterating for the fifth time *sound judgement and calm deliberation* was almost drowned out in a chorus of "name him Fergie," "who is it?" "go it again" and various other encouraging and sarcastic cries, and then we got the thread of the speech again. "I nominate this gentleman as the leader of no party, but as an Independent member of this society. The Federal Party, Mr. President and gentlemen, is not in this election. I have the honour to submit to you the name of Mr. F.C. Perrin." The scene that followed is beyond description. There was hurrying to and fro in the ranks of the Outsiders, and amazement written on every feature. This then was the bomb of the Federals! They were out of the fight, but as a Parthian shot, their astute leader, Prometheus like, had stolen the fire of the Outside party, for be it known to all that the aforesaid Mr. Perrin was the ratified candidate of the Outsiders. The moment was critical, but calm returned to the ranks of the Outside party when a wrathful Jupiter in the form of Mr. C.A. Stuart mounted the platform and nominated Mr. F.E. Perrin. He was followed by the aforesaid fiery element in the form of Mr. Perrin who declined the nomination of Mr. Ferguson and accepted that of the Outside party. The game was now up.[21]

This description shows the formidable political skills Ferguson had even while an undergraduate: personal popularity, ability to deal with hecklers, and the astuteness necessary to make the most of even a hopeless political cause – and all of this within the walls of the Literary and Scientific Society. It was this sort of example of direct political connection between student experience and later life that the Lit. tried to foster and enhance by moving to party politics. It should be noted that C.A. Stuart, Ferguson's opponent at that meeting, was himself elected to be an officer of the Lit. and later served for a year (1905) as an MLA in Alberta before becoming a judge. Stuart, too, in his time was an acknowledged a "leader of men."[22]

LEGAL ANIMALS

Stuart and Ferguson, however, were rare beasts indeed; the other political animals of the Lit. in this period proved to be horses of quite a different colour who were largely running a different race than their predecessors had. On 21 October 1902, McGregor Young, professor of constitutional and international law at the University of Toronto, gave the *Varsity* his opinions on the changes in the legal profession and some advice for prospective law students. He noted:

The place of the law student in the new order it is hard to define. Already, the junior partner and the office staff have occupied his ancient field, and it is abundantly clear that the training of his fathers is no longer available – that the student of law must more than ever depend on academic instruction for his professional education. How then can a student of the University best prepare himself for such a calling? ... What is termed the social life – the life beyond the class-rooms and the examination roll – is of peculiar value to the law student. He should take his part in the executive work of the college societies, and make the most of every chance to acquire facility in debate and in expressing his views upon the topics that engage the attention of the student world.[23]

These comments from a gentleman who was also a former officer of the Lit. were taken to heart by many students at University College. Eighty-eight of this cohort went from executive positions on the Lit. into legal careers.

These lawyers were also to learn that the statement "the training of his fathers" could have more meanings than the ones Professor Young specifically intended. For this generation of students, the old ways of operating and the level of success and control over the running of their profession had largely vanished.

For example, only five of the eighty-eight became benchers of the Law Society, somewhat less than the critical mass attained by those of an earlier period. Two of them, Craig McKay and Hugh McLaughlin, were elected in 1941. These two graduated from University College in 1913, and this minor coincidence looks similar to the Crooks-Blake partnership of the 1870s. But McLaughlin and McKay's connections went far beyond the Lit. Hugh McLaughlin's father was an influential and powerful Toronto lawyer from whom he inherited a thriving practice. McKay was the son of S.G. McKay, KC, who had been a life bencher until his death in 1928.[24]

Also generally absent from this group of lawyers was the interconnectedness by marriage that had been so prominent among the Lit. officers in the first period. Only a few of these Lit. officers' siblings show up as spouses of their fellow students. In the new profession of the law kinship networks appear to have declined.

If the lawyers were not prominent in the governance of their profession at Osgoode Hall, what happened to these eighty-eight? Did the Lit. not provide the essential training that McGregor Young suggested it must? The answer appears to be no, but the issues and evidence are not as simple as they were in the earlier period. Forty-five of the lawyers were listed in various editions of *The Canadian Who's Who*, *Who's Who in Canada*, and *Who's Who in America*, a form of public acknowledgment that suggests a degree of prominence generally, if not necessarily in their profession.

How lawyers made their living, though, was changing. Sixteen of the group spent a portion of their careers working for others. Two of these men were lawyers for the Canadian Pacific Railway, and the others were civil servants of one type or another. Ex-officers of the Lit. could also be found at every level of government. Charles M. Colquhon was city solicitor in Toronto, Victor A. Sinclair was chairman of the Worker's Compensation Board of Ontario, and Oliver Mowat Biggar was chief electoral officer in Ottawa. Five Crown attorneys were also counted in this total. In a sense, this new orientation signalled the decline of the "professional gentleman" image of independent practitioners; government employment was now a growing source of opportunity in a developing civil service. The city solicitors, as well, could take some pride in the fact that their role was directly connected to municipal economic development. James Grant Schiller went one step further and combined his law practice with the vice-presidency of the St. Catharines chamber of commerce.[25]

Twelve of the lawyers became businessmen and another two combined their legal practice with large-scale farming operations. The connection between the legal profession and business had been developing for some time before this, but it was increasingly visible around the turn of the twentieth century. This was the era when a lawyer such as Robert Home Smith could move from a legal background into serious entrepreneurial activities such as real estate development and financial investment.[26] The Lit.'s example of a Home Smith was Errel Ironside, who built a significant real estate business before the stock market crash of 1929 destroyed it and led to his suicide.[27] Not all who went into business were that unlucky. Richard V. LeSueur moved to Sarnia, involved himself in the affairs of the local petroleum concerns, and after a short time in Peru emerged as president of Imperial Oil. Harold G. Fox used his knowledge of patent law (in this field, he was referred to as "Canada's doyen") to great success as a manager of a zipper company in St. Catharines.

Neither business nor the civil service guaranteed a successful law career, and four of the ex-officers of the Lit. left the profession, two voluntarily and two by force. The voluntary cases both decided to become writers. The other two were disbarred; the Law Society's crackdown on professional ethics in the 1930s[28] caught them with their hands in the till. Both, however, recovered to pursue business careers.

One thing that did not change in this second cohort was the propensity of members to become judges. Twelve of the eighty-eight attained this position – six in Ontario, two in Alberta, one each in the three other western provinces, and one, Cecil Clegg, in Alaska. These men joined the civil servants and businessmen among a legal elite that had moved increasingly away from interest in the Law Society to focus more on the task of making a living in a changing legal environment.

EDUCATIONAL ANIMALS

The lure of teaching continued to attract ex-officers of the Lit. in the 1891–1921 period. Eighty-one spent at least part of their lives in the teaching profession (this figure includes eight clergymen), a proportion similar to that of the first era. But this second generation switched its preferences for teaching opportunities. Only thirty-five became high school teachers, while forty-four were professors at colleges and universities.

There are at least two good reasons that can be brought forward for the decline in the high school as a location for post-university careers for Lit. men. One of them is the oft-mentioned "feminization" of the Ontario high school system. As Susan Gelman has pointed out, the percentage of women teaching secondary school in Ontario rose from 8.4% in 1881 to 49.8% in 1930.[29] Under these circumstances, it might be that this generation of university-educated men decided not to enter a profession that was no longer considered masculine. The second factor might have been the lack of possible advancement in the profession given the entrenchment of an earlier generation in the school system. One way to show this is to note that the percentage of high school teachers in the 1891–1921 cohort who became principals declined (16 of 35, or 45.7%), compared to the 55% of the earlier period. And the locations where they became principals also shifted: only half of them held their positions in Ontario; the rest went elsewhere. Western Canada was now the preserve of the male high school teacher who had ambitions to administer a school. J.F. MacDonald noted this trend towards "leakage" to the West in a 1909 issue of *Queen's Quarterly*.[30]

With the profession no longer holding out the opportunity of advancement or the guarantee of masculine reinforcement, it is not surprising that for many male graduates teaching became a way-station on the road to other things. Of the thirty-five high school teachers, one resigned to study medicine, three went into business, one became a church worker, and five quit to become professors. This notion of pedagogy as a way-station did not invariably apply, however, as two former Lit. officers gave up their business careers in order to teach.

Another point that bears mentioning is the connection of these teachers to the rise of the civil service. All of them were technically civil servants because their salaries were paid by the various provincial boards of education. But four went the next step, becoming inspectors and superintendents of schools.

On the whole, though, this group of high school teachers does not appear to have had the same degree of cumulative impact on the profession that the early group had. The case was far better for the forty-four who became professors. This generation of post-secondary educators spread far wider than the previous group. Only eight spent the majority of their careers at the University of Toronto (one other, F.B.R. Hellems, resigned over the Dale issue in 1895[31]). Sixteen of them went to the United States – three each to Washington State, California, and Pennsylvania. The remaining twenty stayed in Canada. In this period, the creation of new institutions meant that the opportunities for a university career in Canada were greater than ever before, and ex-Lit. officers could be found at the Universities of Manitoba, Saskatchewan, Alberta, and British Columbia, as well as at McGill, Queen's, McMaster, and the University of Western Ontario.

In the administration of the universities, this generation made great strides. Four of the University of Toronto professors ended up as chairs of departments, a victory for the "nativist" faction at the university.[32] Another eight occupied chairs or headships at other universities. And twelve ascended to the presidencies or principalships of colleges or universities (see table 3.9). Seven of these were theological institutions (Indore College in India included), so this is also partially a list of leadership in the clergy. Together with the deans, these lists comprise twenty-four of forty-four who rose to a high level within the academic hierarchy.

The success rate in post-secondary education can also be demonstrated by the few who quit. Only six abandoned the profession, one to be a civil servant in Washington, DC, one to join the clergy, three to enter business, and one to engage in research. The researcher, John L. Hogg, was a noted academic troublemaker at several Canadian institutions, where his overzealous advocacy of research made him conspicuous and somewhat of a liability, though his research activities in New Jersey were sufficient to gain him an obituary in the *New York Times*.[33] One of the businessmen, George Malcolm Smith, quit as a professor at the University of Toronto to become a stockbroker in 1929. A year later the crash ended that career, whereupon he joined the staff of the University of Alberta and became dean of Arts. Another, William H. Day, found the lucrative possibilities of draining the Holland Marsh north of Toronto to be irresistible, and quit the Ontario College of Agriculture to pursue them. Even the civil servant, Oliver Bowles, only left because his services as a mineral technologist were more appreciated in Washington, DC, than at the University of Minnesota. Most of those departing the profession, thus, did so because they were guaranteed better success elsewhere.

Four of the professors also directly identified themselves as civil servants, adding to the list of professionals who were connected to this growing sector. Two were geologists and two economists. Among the other forty were those who provided advice and opinion to government agencies.

Thirty-four of the professors, over three-quarters of the total, were listed in various who's who directories for their respective countries. Four of them may have been listed for other reasons – one as an engineer, two as civil servants, and one as a clergyman. The other thirty were listed simply as professors. By contrast, only two high school teachers were granted status in the who's who volumes, and both only after they had been named school superintendent. North American high schools were declining in influence compared to the universities, and the careers of ex-officers of the Lit. reflected these trends.

SCIENTIFIC ANIMALS

Another career path related to research. The University of Toronto before 1890 was not a place where scientific research could happily coexist with teaching. However, beginning in the 1890s, A.B. McKillop notes, "social and economic imperatives gave the cause of pure research increasing momentum."[34] Two successive presidents of the university, James Loudon and Robert Falconer, were fervent promoters of research in a university environment.[35] For the entire 1890–1921 period, science was a popular interest of the university's faculty, and by extension of the student body. Nine ex-officers of the Lit. took this lesson to heart, and for a portion of their careers their occupation would be "scientist," one that was unknown to earlier students.

Being a scientist, though, did not connote the same sort of professional independence that attached to other professions. To be a scientist at this time inevitably meant working for other people. Seven of the scientists could also be properly termed civil servants, with the other two more mundanely referred to as employees. The latter two were John C. MacIntosh, an industrial chemist at a northern Ontario mine, and Angus McLeod, who was a geologist in Texas for Shell Oil and who later became a manager of some of their operations. These two industrial scientists represent the beginning of a wave inspired by the growing needs of industry for university-trained researchers.

Among the seven civil servants were five astronomers, one chemist, and a meteorologist. All five of the astronomers worked for the Dominion Observatory of Canada, and two also gave time to the

Geodetic Survey of Canada. As Richard Jarrell notes in his history of astronomy in Canada, "Until quite recently, the story of the training of professional astronomers in Canada is simply the history of the Department of Astronomy, University of Toronto."[36] The astronomy course, begun by Clarence Augustus Chant, himself a Lit. ex-officer who graduated in 1890 and was thus part of the earlier group, began graduating quality students, many of whom went directly to the Dominion Observatory. The five astronomers who were also ex-officers of the Lit. were central to the development of the observatory. That said, a certain degree of political ineptitude can be detected in the careers of three of them, who allowed large amounts of instrumentation to be packed and shipped to the new Dominion Astrophysical Observatory essentially under their noses and without their consent.[37]

Ultimately, three of the five astronomers reached high administrative positions within the Dominion Observatory, William Harper became director; Ralph DeLury, assistant director; and Fergus A. McDiarmid, chief astronomer. John Patterson, director of the Dominion Meteorological Service, can be added to this group that represented a degree of scientific leadership no less impressive than the political leadership provided by George H. Ferguson. These four, as well as astronomer Robert Motherwell, were recognized by the editors of the *Canadian Who's Who*. Patterson is also notable as one of the leading figures in the fight for the creation of a scientific research journal in Canada.[38]

A scientific career, then, was increasingly chosen by the ex-officers of the Literary and Scientific Society in this period, ironically just before the group jettisoned the "Scientific" from its name.[39] And such research was not restricted to those who left the academy. Some who stayed, like Eli F. Burton and Lachlan Gilchrist, made their own contributions to the progress of pure research.[40] The activities of the Lit. in the 1890–1921 period were not designed to produce men of science, but the university environment was sufficient to overcome this liability in the society's organization.

By the last decade of the nineteenth century engineering was in transition toward a new emphasis on advanced education, and perhaps even professional certification, for those entering engineering careers, those in control of educational institutions, and those interested in science both in its pure and applied forms.[41] In the latter category were James Loudon and Adam Crooks, who supported the creation of engineering courses and who especially welcomed the creation of the SPS and its location near the University of Toronto.[42]

Loudon was not the only one who welcomed this proximity. The Literary and Scientific Society also extended a warm welcome to the engineering students, and set aside two positions on their executive, from 1885 to the turn of the century, to be filled by students from the SPS. This arrangement may have come about as the result of the willingness of engineering students to participate in the organization of the Literary Society's Conversazione in 1885.[43] These seats were not filled every year; nevertheless, thirty engineering students can be counted among the ex-officers of the Lit. during this period. There are, however, only twenty known engineers and three surveyors in this cohort. And of these twenty engineers, two did not have an engineering degree, another example of the curious nature of the profession of engineering at this time (this means, as well, that the careers of nine engineering students are not known).

For the twenty men about whom I was able to locate information, ten were civil engineers, four were electrical engineers, and two were mining engineers. This spread highlights the dominance of civil engineering among the choices available for prospective students in the late nineteenth and early twentieth centuries. Four did not end their careers in engineering; two quit to sell insurance, one became a manufacturer, and the other two entered the related field of architecture. The sixteen that stayed in the profession were split evenly between independent workers and employees of others. Six became civil servants, working as city engineers and provincial engineers, and two were civil engineers for the Canadian National Railway. The others ran their own companies or partnerships.

One of the growing issues in the literature on engineering in the late nineteenth and early twentieth centuries is the relative strengths and weakness of the various bodies agitating for professional certification. J. Rodney Millard has shown that the Canadian Society of Civil Engineers (CSCE), founded in 1887, had pretensions similar to the Law Society of Upper Canada. A learned society with high educational requirements for admission, the CSCE sought to raise the standards of professional practice in the field and agitated for legislation that would limit the profession to a closed group.[44] Unlike the Law Society the CSCE did not have much success, because it was perceived to be a small Montreal-dominated group that did not have the best interests of the profession at heart. Also, engineer-surveyors in Ontario were already represented by the Association of Ontario Land Surveyors (AOLS), which had gained the status of a closed professional society in 1892.

Other than belonging to the AOLS, Gidney and Millar argue, engineers were too mobile a group to care about professional organization in the late nineteenth and early twentieth centuries.[45] Indeed, only three joined the AOLS, two of whom were practising land surveyors in Ontario. The third, railway engineer John Chalmers of Rat Portage and Winnipeg, quit the AOLS when he joined the public service in

Edmonton, Alberta. Although James S. Dobie rose to become president of the AOLS in 1913 and served many years as a councillor after that, he was the only one among former officers of the Lit. to exercise leadership in the profession of land surveying. By contrast, twelve of the twenty engineers were listed as members of the Engineering Institute of Canada (the successor body to the CSCE) in 1928. Considering that only fifteen of the twenty were still in Canada at that date, this was an impressive percentage. Not one of them, however, had joined the organization before 1902, and only three had joined before 1907. Three engineers did serve as councillors on the governing body of the Institute, but the first of these, Donald A. Ross, did not attain his position until 1916. Gidney and Millar's hypothesis about the professionalizing of engineering can thus be illustrated by the activities of these ex-officers. None of them was in a hurry to join a professional-defence organization or to promote the interests of such an organization at a leadership level. They were, on the whole, more interested in simply working as engineers.

Five of the twenty achieved fame in the *Canadian Who's Who*. Two of these were city engineers, in Niagara Falls and Saskatoon respectively. The Niagara Falls city engineer, Charles H. Mitchell, was destined for a greater career as a general in the First World War, after which he became dean of engineering at the University of Toronto; his first listing in a who's who, though, was simply as the Niagara Falls city engineer. Of the remaining three, two were consulting engineers – one joined Ontario Hydro while the other (Ernest Neelands) was a mining engineer and global traveller. The last, Donald A. Ross, did not end up in the *Canadian Who's Who* until he began serious work as an architect in the 1940s. Another of the twenty, James C. Johnston, might have ended up in the who's who of any of the United States, Australia, or smaller South American countries if he had stayed in one place long enough, but his status as an "internationally-renowned expert on highway construction" kept him on the road for most of his life. In this respect he too was a typical engineer of the early twentieth century: mobile, hard-working, and not interested in taking on any sort of professional leadership.

RELIGIOUS ANIMALS

Despite indications that between 1891 and 1921 Canada was evolving into a more secular society under the pressures of industrialization and scientific thought, a large number of ex-officers of the Lit. pursued careers in the clergy. The group was far less diverse in terms of religious

orientation than the earlier cohort, with thirty-seven beginning as Presbyterians, thirteen as Anglicans, and two as Congregationalists. Much
of this absence of diversity can be most probably attributed to the
entry of Victoria College into federation with the university in 1887.
This allowed Methodists to reap the benefits of the University of
Toronto staff without actually having to attend University College, and
the theologically-minded appear to have taken that route. Anglicans,
however, did not head to Trinity with the same regularity, and the
connection between Wycliffe College and University College forged in
the 1870s allowed Anglicans contemplating the ministry to continue
to be members of the Literary and Scientific Society.

The Lit., however, was still not permitted to discuss religious affairs,
and although it continued to identify itself as a possible training
ground for pulpit orators its impact on members' religious thought
remains impenetrable. Few of the ex-officers of the Lit., for example,
can be connected with one of the primary religious currents of the era,
the development of the "social gospel"; only three are known to have
had a direct connection to that movement. James A. Miller took on
the position of supervisor of immigration and migration in Ontario
for the Presbyterian Church, Robert F. Thompson quit active preaching
to oversee Unemployment Relief in Ottawa, and Claris Silcox headed
up the Social Service Council and became a noted social and religious
researcher. Beyond that, there is no real sign that the other forty-nine
were interested in the proclamation of God's kingdom on earth.[46]

One would also have expected more of the products of a "godless"
college to have embraced and supported the movement for church
union. All but one of the thirty-seven Presbyterians survived into the
union period; twenty-one of them joined the United Church, while
sixteen did not. John Webster Grant notes that "an overwhelming
majority" of the Presbyterian ministry joined the United Church, leaving the Presbyterian Church in Canada "bereft of ministers and organization."[47] A less-than-overwhelming majority of the ex-Lit. officers
who became ministers followed this route. The individual motivation
and local circumstances of the church union movement have not been
studied in any great detail, but one interesting point can be noted here.
Two of those who stayed in the Presbyterian Church were nominated
as moderator during the course of their lives, while none of the United
Church converts achieved such a height. Even in local synodical and
conference leadership, the Presbyterians from University College outnumbered the United Church members. The tenuous possibility exists
that the decision by so many of this group to remain with the Presbyterians was based on the same sort of close calculation that had led

to victory at Lit. elections; that is to say, they opted to be big fish in the smaller Presbyterian pond rather than to fight Victoria College's Methodists for power within the larger group.

This possibility can be balanced against another that has been suggested by N. Keith Clifford in *The Resistance to Church Union in Canada, 1904–1939*. Clifford notes that the struggle to preserve the Presbyterian Church in Canada was a logical outgrowth of the disestablishment of the Canadian churches in the 1850s. By resisting the call for a "national crusade" as supported by church unionists, those who remained Presbyterian were affirming a "major effect of disestablishment: religious pluralism."[48] University College itself was created as part of the process of disestablishment in the 1850s, and its status as a secular institution and the diversity of religious backgrounds of its students can also be seen as part of this pluralist philosophy. Students at University College may have been more sensitive to the rights of different religious groups for separate existence, and this may account in large measure for the greater percentage of them staying in the Presbyterian Church.

Still strong was the tendency to combine clerical office with the editorship of publications. In the 1920s and 1930s, the editors of the *Canadian Churchman, The Congregationalist,* and Presbyterian Publications were all former Lit. members. So, too, was the director of publicity for the United Church from 1925 to 1929. Support for missionary movements at home and abroad can also be noted in the careers of a few. But, on the whole, there were more who spent their careers solely as ministers, without seeking the other roles available in church organizations. Twenty-five of the fifty-two clergymen were content just to preach, a higher figure than in the previous period. This may represent a return to stability in the ministry after the confusions of the latter nineteenth century.

More clerics also stayed in Canada. Only two ended up in the United States – Wm. Gilroy in Boston and George Logie in Arizona. Four spent time as foreign missionaries abroad – two in China, one in India, and one in Japan. On the whole, though, Canada was now seen as a large enough place to accommodate most of the clergy produced by local institutions. Twenty-two even achieved fame in the *Canadian Who's Who*. Four of these men were there by virtue of their position as principals of theological colleges, and a few others were only mentioned in the 1912 edition and then never after; however, the proportion is still significant. Although their names are not prominent in the books discussing the debates on theological change and social development in Canada, contemporary observers believed they were important contributors to Canadian society.

NEW ANIMALS

Four accountants, three life insurance salesmen, and six actuaries were also among the ex-officers of the Lit. in this period. They represent a nebulous and barely studied group of nascent professionals emerging in early twentieth-century Canada. These graduates, like the astronomers, found themselves in professions in which counting, and thus a degree of numeracy, was helpful.

Helpful, but not expected. Among the thirteen we find seven graduates in math and physics and one in chemistry, but also one political science graduate, a philosophy major, and even a student who graduated in classics. There was no direct connection, then, between mathematical skill and a career as an accountant or actuary in this period. For accountants, especially, it seems to have been experience, rather than university training, that allowed one to claim professional status. Two of the accountants only advanced to that rank after serving as clerks in the civil service of Canada. Charles J. Allen moved from being a clerk with the auditor-general's department to working as an audit accountant; Cassius Campbell emerged from a position as clerk with the Department of Railways and Canals to become an accountant with the Department of Finance and later chief of the currency division of the Bank of Canada. The other two accountants were not civil servants, one of them being an accountant with the Presbyterian Church until church union, and the other, William D. Love, becoming a chartered accountant in Winnipeg with interests in investment and real estate as well. Love was the only one of the four to become a CA, a designation that appears not to have established itself in Canada until later in the twentieth century.

Actuaries in this period were almost indistinguishable from life insurance agents, and the emergence of actuarial science as a profession is hard to document. Several of the ex-Lit. officers who entered the profession strove to change that relative obscurity. They were two recognized societies to which they could turn, the American Institute of Actuaries (AIA), and the Actuarial Society of America (ASA). Both societies were dedicated to the promotion of actuarial science and both held annual examinations by which they certified new members.[49] Although the AIA was the older organization and allowed Canadians to join, it was the ASA that received the first loyalty of this group of actuaries. Each ex-officer-turned-actuary joined the ASA within a year or two of graduation from university. Five joined the AIA at some later period, ranging from a gap of three years for John McKellar to a span of thirty-two years for John Spencer Thompson.

Two former Lit. officers rose to leadership in the ASA. John Spencer Thompson was on the council of the organization from 1917 to 1950, serving as editor, secretary, vice-president, and, ultimately, president from 1932 to 1933. In 1924, Thompson represented the United States government at the tenth international conference of actuaries held in Rome. John M. Laird of Connecticut General Life was touted at his death as a leader among professional actuaries, and he succeeded Thompson as editor of publications for the ASA in 1922, serving until 1936. Professional leadership among actuaries was clearly yet another route for ex-Lit. officers. This possibility also existed at a local level. Charles H. Armstrong was among the early members of the Actuaries Club of Toronto, and served as its secretary in 1917.[50]

The ex-officers of the Lit. who embarked on careers in life insurance had one other thing in common. All but one of them managed thirty-to-forty year careers in the business, a degree of job stability that was remarkable considering that many of their careers intersected with the Great Depression (see table 3.10). The one whose career was most choppy was John McKellar, who both suffered from occasional ill-nesses and also married a famous organist, Gertrude Fritts. Her career path, which involved significant travel, made his own less stable.

The men who entered the actuarial field were all employed in different companies. No attempt seems to have been made by ex-officers of the Lit. to hire each other. Given the stability of the careers of the actuaries listed above, however, a case can be made that university-trained actuaries had advantages conferred by their degrees that made such connections unnecessary. A new opportunity for employment had opened up in twentieth-century Canada, and an increasing number of university graduates pursued it, being supported in time by a university program (commerce) that was dedicated to the professional choices of accountancy and actuarial science.

Kilgour, Laird, McKellar, Reid, and Wood received listings in the *Canadian Who's Who*. Their notices attest to the fact that in this field, just as in the law, academia, and others, leadership could be recognized nationally and that those in the business were equally public men.

CIVIL SERVICE ANIMALS

An increasing number of professional men could also be classified as civil servants. But the impact of the civil service on university graduates was broader. Indeed, there were observers of the university scene in this period who believed that the civil service was a significant career path for students to consider. As A.S. Sibbald pointed out in the *University of Toronto Monthly* in 1910:

There are those who figure in the stress and struggle of party warfare, whose names are household terms and whose deeds and policies form the topic of engrossing conversation in the city and the country. The white light of publicity is ever directed towards them, and it is only natural that the college man should – as do all others – tend to confuse public men with party service and to regard the fields of public service and of party warfare as being one and the same. Such a view is untenable. The University graduate, if debarred from such a life by either distaste or incapacity for it, would do well to remember that engaging in party warfare is not only and may possibly not be the best means by which he can serve the community. In the immense field of government administration there is an increasing number of opportunities for thoroughly well-trained men. The civil service is worthy of at least the careful consideration of the University graduate.[51]

In the occupations already examined the civil service played a role. But there were still thirteen other ex-officers of the Lit. who spent significant time as civil servants.

Five doctors, for instance, lent their expertise to various governmental agencies. Four of them worked, as might be anticipated, as coroners. One of these, John W. McIntosh, combined the role of coroner with that of Indian superintendent on Manitoulin Island. The fifth, William A. Groves, served seven years as a pension commissioner in Winnipeg, while also presumably continuing to practise medicine.

The other major source of civil service experience was in geological surveying and mine inspection. This occupied four of the former student leaders of University College. Sibbald had pointed out that careers in the civil service did not offer as much remuneration as a successful business career,[52] and two of those in the mining and geology field discovered this early, one leaving to become a wool merchant and the other to go into advertising. This left four other cases. One of them, Frederick J. Lyle, gave up his tanning business to become trade and industry director in Ontario's Department of Planning and Development. Another, Arthur S. Bleakney (whose father was also a civil servant) became a trade commissioner for Canada in various countries. The remaining two became managers of Ontario government agencies, Edward Ashworth at Ontario Hydro and Arthur Birmingham at the LCBO.

The civil service was not a well-trod path toward national recognition. Although five of those in this group did get listings in the *Canadian Who's Who*, only two of them received this recognition because they were civil servants. Birmingham was noted as a political organizer in 1912, but never received a listing while he worked for the LCBO. Lachlan Burwash and Wiliam E.H. Carter were only listed because of their skill as engineers, not as public servants. That left Edward Ashworth and Harold C. Cooke, both of whom were recognized as civil servants in their entries, but only as secondary to their achievements as an engineer and a geologist respectively.

In this respect, Sibbald anticipated matters when he declared, "While the populace bows down before its idols of the platform and of the spoken word, while the cheering and the shouting go to those upon whom falls the more spectacular work of government, the civil servant goes his way, doing a work none the less deserving because comparatively unrecognised ... An honourable profession, interesting work and congenial surroundings – this is what the civil service offers – this, and the epitaph that one has tried to serve his country."[53] The epitaph was one with which increasing numbers of university graduates would be satisfied.

PUBLIC MEN

The bewildering array of possible careers open to university graduates of this period was not limited to those discussed above. Nothing has been said about most of the doctors, journalists, and businessmen, let alone the failed Shakespearean actor and the secretary-treasurer of the Ontario Motor League. However, the categories covered above should highlight certain points about the careers of the ex-officers of the Lit. from 1891 to 1921. A sizable number were still entering the traditional talking professions of law, education, and the clergy. These professions were, however, changing, and the types of career pursued in this period were in some cases distinctly different from those of the first generation. Beyond the traditional professions, however, were some new, emerging career choices in science, engineering, and even actuarial work that could be put forward as legitimate alternatives for those wishing to promote the prosperity and advancement of Canada as a modern, industrial nation.

As well, the ex-officers of the Lit. showed in this period that they had confused the issues of the day while they were students. They had redesigned their administrative and governmental structures in order to promote Canadian politics in the belief that their services would be badly needed as political leaders. In doing so, they failed to create circumstances that would encourage most of them to enter the political arena after they graduated from university. It is possible that the twelve students from the era of direct political activity who died during the First World War might have all become politicians, but certainly the seventy-nine who survived made little attempt to. Those University College students that did end up in high political office after graduation normally had no experience on the executive of the Lit., with the possible exception of George Howard Ferguson.

In search of political training, however, the officers of the Lit. did succeed in gaining a notion of what was expected of them in the future. As my numerous references to the who's who volumes attest, these students did become, in the years to follow, *public* men if not *political* men. In the rough and tumble of Ontario politics around the turn of the century, as the Liberals were increasingly in the public eye because of their electoral corruption,[54] it seemed only natural to expect that an infusion of civilized university graduates would improve matters. By the time the changes required at the university to produce these men were accomplished, however, they were not as necessary as they had seemed at the height of the crisis. The ex-officers of the Lit. had, however, in the process discovered things about the Canadian political scene that quite probably allowed them to enjoy careers more attuned to the needs of Canada than those of the earlier Professional Gentleman whose focus was so narrowly fixed on the Law Society of Upper Canada.

4 The Silent Ones: Women, 1891–1921

ORIGINS AND DESTINATIONS

Writing the history of nineteenth- and early twentieth-century university students is a strenuous task that involves dealing with a vast silence. University women, however, form an even more troublesome subset. As Jo LaPierre noted in her work on the first generation of Canadian female students, "Women slipped so silently into the classrooms of Canadian universities that they left remarkably little record of their presence ... As a result they seem to have made themselves almost invisible."[1]

Those who have studied the early generations of women who attended university have generally not engaged in any quantitative work as to their origins.[2] However, University College authorities collected the same information on their female students as they did on the males, and what they did not collect can be found in vital statistics collected by various government agencies. Marks and Gaffield have shown the intricate connections that can be drawn from quantitative records of early university women and the milieu in which they lived and studied.[3] Their conclusions match to a great degree my findings about officers of the Women's Literary Society and Women's Undergraduate Association from 1891 to 1921. Judith Fingard's quantitative work on Dalhousie University students also shows certain patterns similar to those of University College.[4] For instance, both Fingard's research and the Marks and Gaffield study note that women were more likely than men to come from the city in which the institution they attended was located. For Queen's University the figure was 35% for women as opposed to 16% for men, a ratio of two to one.[5] Fingard notes that two-thirds of the Dalhousie women in the first generation and half in the second generation came from Halifax; she does not, however, give comparative data for the male population.[6] The birthplaces of the officers of the WUA and the Lit. were similar in pattern: 37% of the women came from Toronto as opposed to 26% of the men during the same period (see table 4.1).

In terms of parental occupation, the women of this cohort differed from those described in the Dalhousie and Queen's studies. Fingard notes that her data cannot be used to draw absolute conclusions, as she was unable to locate parental occupations for 30% of her second-generation students and for almost all of the first-generation ones. What she did find for the second generation was that 30% were daughters of businessmen and professionals, while 6% were daughters of working men or farmers, a five-to-one ratio.[7] The Queen's study found that two-thirds of women at the university had fathers from "higher-status occupations," while only 48% of the men were in the same situation. Farmer's children at Queen's made up 21% of all female students and 37% of all male students.[8] Compared to this, the women at University College who served as student leaders were somewhat different. A greater percentage of them had fathers who were businessmen and professionals than did the men, but not strikingly more. The most significant difference was in the proportion of farm women attending the college (see table 4.2).

Another point needs to be made about parental origins of WLS/WUA women. There were twelve lawyers, fifteen medical men, nine clerics, and thirteen academics among the fathers of these women. In percentage terms, this was essentially the same distribution as for the contemporary men. There seems no reason to believe that the daughters of professional men at University College were in any way better off financially than their sons. No great difference either can be found among the business backgrounds of the respective parental groups.

In terms of religious affiliation, the most significant difference between the male and female students is that among women the proportion of Presbyterians exceeded 50%, somewhat higher than among the men and above the general level at University College. This difference seems, however, to be directly related to the number of unknown cases – for some reason it was easier to identify the women's religious backgrounds. Beyond the Presbyterians, the general distribution of women among denominations was the same. Indeed, the rough equality between female and male students in terms of religious affiliation at University College suggests that some unseen hand was looking after the thorny question of denominational intermarriage at a "godless" institution (see table 4.3).

All previous studies of women at Canadian universities have noted the tension between those who accepted traditional social roles and those who believed "that women should achieve something 'significant' with their degrees in the larger world, just as men were expected to."[9] The occupational choices available to women seemed limited. As Elsinore McPherson noted in 1920, "Twenty years ago there was only one assured future to which a women graduate could look forward – that of teaching."[10] Alice Massey echoed McPherson's point the same year, commenting that "Hundreds enter the teaching profession not because they are specially gifted to teach, but because there is no means of finding other work suited to their gifts."[11] Although some strides had been made in expanding the range of professions to which women could aspire, the standard options for female Arts graduates remained marriage or teaching.

These limitations are reflected in both the occupational intentions of WLS and WUA officers in this period and the courses of study they pursued while at University College. In both cases there were significant differences from the men of the Lit.

I successfully located admission forms for 87 of the 211 students in this cohort. In forty-two of the cases, intended occupation was left blank. For the forty-five who did fill in the space, thirty-eight responded with "teaching," with the remaining seven spread among "medicine," "dietician," "musician," "missionary," and "secretarial." It is not clear whether the high rate of missing responses was because women were not asked the question or because they failed to respond to it. The response rate was, though, higher for WLS/WUA officers than for students at Queen's University who were asked the same question. Gaffield and Marks found that "the uncertainty regarding future careers among women varied by the student's background," and to some extent this is also true for the University College data. Fifty-four percent of the female students with professional or business backgrounds at University College did not identify their post-graduation plans, compared with 83% at Queen's. Forty-one percent of all other female students were similarly unsure at University College, 42% at Queen's.[12]

A SEPARATED SPHERE

Options were limited for University College women not only in terms of expectations, but also in terms of their academic studies in the Faculty of Arts. Table 4.4 shows the courses of study pursued by WLS/ WUA officers during this period, compared with the percentages of Lit.

members in the same programs. Over half of the women were enrolled in the English and moderns department, compared to only 7% of the men. The top honours programs for male students – political science, philosophy, and maths – occupied 51.5% of the men and only 10% of the women. With the exception perhaps of classics, there was a clear division between women's and men's subjects. Men also had a greater variety of programs open to their enrolment – 6.9% of the men were in programs from which women were absent.

For a reference point, table 4.5 shows the courses of study for arts students at University College for 1912–13. In that year there were five programs that had only men in them, compared to just one populated solely by women. The percentages of men and women in respective split courses are similar to those of the figures in table 4.4. Tables 4.4 and 4.5 also point out some other interesting facts about the differing experiences of men and women at University College. Unlike Bessie Scott, the by-now mythologized early woman student of University College, many women at the college did not have to give up their "beloved math."[13]

Certainly there were limitations as to what women could study at University College, even if these were not expressly stated in the calendar. The combination of lower expectations and reduced choice as to course of study was a dual attack that none of the male students had to face. This gender dichotomy leads naturally to the point that beyond any notion of a "separate sphere" was another principle of a "separated sphere": women were faced with curricular as well as extracurricular separation. Coeducation was allegedly in place at University College, but the practical reality was that equal access was at least another generation away.

Popular student culture reflected that situation. In 1887, the University of Toronto *Song Book* contained among its songs "suitable for use in the drawing-room and around the camp-fire" a piece entitled "The Maid from Algoma." Among the two versions of the lyrics published were the following stanzas:

"What are your studies, my pretty maid?"
Heave away, heigho, heigho
"Chinese and Quaternions, sir," she said,
"And I come away back from Algoma."

"Then who will marry you, my pretty maid?"
Heave away, heigho, heigho
"Cultured girls don't marry, sir," she said,
"And I go away back to Algoma."[14]

As if to show the confusion as to what would become of the educated female graduate, the song also has a second version, in which the "maid" confidently replies with the name of the person she will marry. These lyrics demonstrate the ambiguity of coeducation, but also reveal its truth. Women graduates faced one key life choice that constricted all their others. They could either marry, or they could not.

In the late nineteenth and early twentieth centuries, this uneasy balance between marriage and university education was occasionally talked about, and in the case of the Domestic Science movement it was used as the basis for an educational philosophy. Echoing the taunts of the U.C. *Song Book*, Adelaide Hoodless, the prime mover behind domestic science, declared:

Surely mental development could be secured on lines bearing more directly upon matters relating to social and domestic laws, with which women must deal. That a trained mind is desirable in the proper regulation of domestic matters we must admit, but whether the solution of a problem in "Harmonium Progression" or the translation of "Bellum Gallicum" will prove more conducive to the comfort and happiness of the home than the scientific knowledge of sanitation, food values, care of the sick, artistic furnishing, the management of children, etc., remain to be proved.[15]

Or, in short, "'Cultured girls don't marry, sir.'" Hoodless's opinion that home economics classes for women should be mandatory did not make much headway at University College, which understood that university education was not designed for the production of wives and mothers. The maids of Algoma, however, faced tremendous societal pressure to follow traditional roles.

MARRIAGE AND FAMILY LIFE

One hundred twenty-four of 211 of the WLS and WUA officers are known to have married. Seventy are known to have remained single (or at least were still unmarried at the age of 60), and in the remaining seventeen cases no data are available either way. If these latter cases are counted as unmarried, 59% of the WLS/WUA officers married. If they are not counted, the figure rises to 67%.

Fingard found that for her first generation of Dalhousie women between 45% and 59% were married, while for the second generation 55% were married.[16] Gaffield and Marks note that 58% of their Queen's students married, "slightly higher than that of American university women at the time, but ... much lower than the Canadian proportion of 88 per cent for all women in the same age group."[17]

McPherson noted that of the over 3,000 graduates she could find information on, only 33.65% were married, less than the 49.69% of all women in Canada over ten years of age who were noted as married in the 1911 census.[18] These figures are low because McPherson added together all female graduates, including those from years proximate to her research. Women who did marry normally waited a few years before doing so, and because of the great number of female graduates in the 1910–20 period, McPherson's data were skewed.

This capacity for error in marriage rates was well understood by another contemporary observer of university women. In 1929 Margaret Ray "selected a period dating back fifteen years from the present day, on the assumption that if people have any claim to distinction they ought to show signs of it in fifteen years." This fifteen-year rule also covered most of the marriages among university women. Ray showed for the class of 1914 that 45 of 101 graduates were married, and claimed that this held true for almost every graduating year before or after.[19] A slight challenge to this trend can be found in the forty-year reports of the University College classes of 1902 and 1903, which reported that 57% of all living women graduates from those years were married.[20]

Whether we accept the figure of married university women as 45% or 59%, however, the dilemma remains the same. While much has been written about those female graduates who entered the workforce, there is a large black hole in the literature where the role of married women in Canada should be discussed. Gaffield and Marks say merely "most of these women fulfilled the domestic role and that the university served as a precursor to marriage," although they do acknowledge that there is a hidden story of volunteer contributions.[21] Fingard gives some idea of the type of people female graduates married, and she cites marriage as a factor in the out-migration of women from the Maritimes. But she, as well, spends more time talking about the women who had careers outside the home than those who remained within the domestic sphere.[22]

Are somewhere between 45% and 60% of all female graduates of Canadian universities in this period forever to languish in unexamined obscurity because the current scholarly agenda finds them too difficult to track down? Is there any way to evaluate marriage as a contribution to Canadian societal development by educated women?

This problem dogged Margaret Ray in 1929, when she had to concede that she could find only about fifteen female graduates of the University of Toronto who had distinguished themselves on the Canadian scene as a whole. One of her male friends jeered to her, "what a sad array of failures," at which point Ray noted "then indeed my indignation burst its bonds, and the patient seeker-after-truth became transformed into a livid feminist." Among her pointed questions at that point was "How many of the 45% engaged in that most difficult of all partnerships – matrimony – get the credit for the share they have contributed to their husband's success?"[23] This conviction that feminism had an equal obligation to defend married women has been lost in recent literature. To Ray, however, this was a crusade. As she remarked in the next instalment of her study:

Take matrimony, for instance, the most popular of the professions. It may be man's avocation but undoubtably it is woman's vocation. He may furnish the income and put on the storm windows – but change places with your wife and you'll find what a small contribution you have been making to the profession of home-making ... You, in common with the majority of men, maintain that a woman's place is in the home. By your standards the college women cannot be a failure when almost half of them in every year marry and keep up "the sanctity of the home." You feared that if you allowed woman a higher education she would grow economically independent of men, and learn to despise the art of home-making. Well, your fears have not been realized, because education, instead of making women "unwomanly" as you were so fond of predicting, has merely developed her inherent qualities, and as a result made her a more intelligent and more understanding wife and mother ... As long as women are women the majority of them will give first place to the profession of homemaking, although they may not confine themselves exclusively to that one occupation. Any woman ... who has helped her husband in his profession, made his home a comfortable and attractive refuge from business worries, and has borne and brought up a family of children, steering them past the pitfalls of measles, mumps, and a score of childish diseases, as well as the more grave spiritual dangers which beset their lives – any women who has done all this ... and still finds time to be intelligent on matters of public concern, and charming to her husband and friends – well, the man who has the audacity to term her a failure has scarcely the mental equipment of a moron.[24]

This long declaration set the essential parameters for future discussions. There *was* value in the contributions of married university-educated women, and it could be determined by the character of their husbands and the number of their children.

The occupations of the husbands of the WLS/WUA former officers are shown in table 4.6. Of the 124 who married, I was able to determine the occupations for 97 of their first husbands. Seventy of the 124 husbands were university graduates or in professions for which a university education was required. Most of these were University of Toronto graduates (six were Lit. officers), but McGill, Dalhousie, and the Ontario Agricultural College also supplied husbands for these women. None are known to have come from Queen's or the University of Western Ontario, and the Queen's graduate lists are available and complete to as late as 1914. The circle in which these women could locate suitable mates was clearly small.

The women in this cohort married a variety of men. Among the educationalists, all but one were university professors. The businessmen included three bank managers, the president of a bond company, and one industrialist. The lowest rank among the twenty-seven businessmen would probably be the two salesmen; however, both of these were married to post-war WLS/WUA officers and may belong to a trend of the next generation. In general, the women graduates who decided to marry aspired to find middle-class mates and achieved this goal. And, indeed, many of their husbands were quite successful in their careers. Some of them, such as John Spencer Thompson and John Melvin Laird, have been mentioned in chapter 3. Also notable were Ronald Fairbairn McWilliams (a Peterborough lawyer who rose to be the lieutenant-governor of Manitoba); Llewelyn Evans Davis of the Anglican Church; professors Edward A. Bott, William Kilbourne Stewart, and W.P.M. Kennedy; and engineer Robert W. Angus. All of these gentlemen, and many others not listed, lived successful lives and enjoyed fruitful careers.

The great unknown question that plagues this analysis, however, is to what extent the women were responsible for their husbands' successes. Few of the married women received obituaries that adequately account for their roles. Likewise, none of the obituaries for the husbands tell much about the role of their wives in building a sustaining partnership. Only one woman has been the subject of a biography, the remarkable Margaret May Stovel McWilliams, who married the aforementioned lieutenant-governor. In dealing with the McWilliams' lives, Mary Kinnear spends six pages discussing the nature of their relationship. She adroitly points out that while Ronald McWilliams was efficiently destroying both his political career and law practice in Peterborough, Margaret stuck by him, and that she also supported his career-saving move to Winnipeg. Kinnear quotes Ronald as saying that the cool reception his wife was given in Peterborough was also responsible for the relocation. "I brought to Peterborough the ablest woman the town has even known but the animosities toward me were carried into social life against her as well and she spent seven years without being given an opportunity to put her talents to any use whatever," Ronald later declared.[25] Indirectly, then, he could use the treatment accorded his wife as a spur toward leaving town. The two "got along together very well" and, in Kinnear's analysis, it was Margaret's remarkable intellect that kept Ronald moving forward. One relative is quoted as saying that "Ronald never would have got to first base without her."[26] Margaret May Stovel McWilliams would have been an ideal example of Margaret Ray's successful woman graduate as wife.

Beyond this one anecdotal case, however, there seems no decent way to register the effects of marrying a university-educated woman as opposed to any other. Certainly there are cases in which women without university educations were married to successful lawyers and politicians, even in Peterborough and Manitoba. Many officers of the Lit. of the same period, to cite examples close at hand, enjoyed distinguished future careers even though they were married to women who lacked university training.

Eighty-four of the 124 known married women had a total of 187 children (see table 4.7); – one-third are listed as having no children at all. The University of Toronto, however, only made sporadic attempts in this period to collect information on alumni's children. By the 1920s it was publishing regular birth columns in the *Monthly*, but finding birth notices for earlier periods is difficult. Many of these women, as well, did not have their deaths recorded in any university source, so the death notices that would have listed their children cannot be located. Further to that, when death notices are found they often list only surviving children. All of this means that the number of children given in table 4.7 should be treated as a low figure that will no doubt rise as further information is found. Even if more children are located, however, it seems unlikely the figures will increase by the twenty-four children that would have allowed this generation to claim to have reproduced itself. Emily Nett provides figures showing that the fertility rate for the cohort of women born in 1894 was 3,500 per 1,000 women, or 3.5 children per woman.[27] If those figures held for this generation of WLS/WUA officers, they would have produced over 700 offspring; even if only married women are counted, the number would have been over 400.

The general lack of children produced by university-graduated women conforms to the expectations of those who study the Canadian family. Nett cites 17.7% childlessness among married women born between 1906 and 1911, and gives a similar figure for the 1980s, noting that "[child]-free couples are disproportionately concentrated in the upper socio-economic levels. They have high education and are less religious compared to couples with children."[28] The WLS/WUA officers fit neatly into the group that could be expected to produce relatively few offspring or none at all. Anecdotally, this was certainly true for the McWilliams.

For comparative purposes, table 4.8 shows the percentages of the Lit. officers from the 1891–1921 period who became fathers and those who did not. Given the caveats listed above, it appears that more ex-Lit. men than ex-WLS/WUA women remained childless. However, once children were decided upon the former Lit. members produced more offspring than did the WLS/WUA graduates.

Margaret Ray most likely did not have these figures in front of her when she made her analyses in 1929/30. It is not known to what extent the community at large knew the disparity between the size of families of university women and the rest of the Canadian population, and what their opinion might have been on this. Certainly, a case could have been made that these intelligent women were, by producing fewer children, denying Canadian society the benefit of their superior education by passing it on to many more children, but this cannot yet be proven.[29]

Ray's declaration in 1929/30 set the parameters which society could use to evaluate female graduates. Attempts to belittle their contributions to Canadian society either by open derision or deliberate exclusion from scholarly work must be avoided whenever possible. Given the limited data that have been located to date, the present study can only hint at possible lines of analysis, while hoping that they will be aggressively followed up in the future.

CAREERS OUTSIDE THE HOME

Tables 4.9 and 4.10 list the occupation categories and geographical locations of the WLS/WUA officers from 1891 to 1921. These data are generally poor. In many cases this is due to uncertainty regarding dates of marriage and actual status in marriage. Many of those listed as "unknown" in these tables probably should be recorded as "married/housewife," but unless they were certain to have been performing this role I have resisted coding them as such. Geographical location was only coded for a married woman if it was certain she lived in the same place as her husband, a fact that was not always possible to ascertain. These problems become more serious as more time passes, so by thirty years after graduation the amount of unknown data reaches close to 50%. And some of the known data are impossible to judge accurately. The figures for location in Toronto, not surprisingly, are very high, and excellent communications with northeastern US universities made it easier to track former officers who worked there or who were married to professors there. But elsewhere, especially in western Canada and the US Midwest, university women seem to have disappeared and cannot be clearly tracked. This was even true eighty years ago. In 1920

McPherson was unable to find data on many University College female graduates. Of the 1,271 women graduates to 1917, 378, or nearly 30%, were listed as "unaccounted for."[30] This highlights the difficulty of retrieving quantitative information on women university graduates.

A close study of McPherson's work on the careers of Canadian university women outlines the general pattern by which WLS/WUA officers can be analyzed. Her figures on University College show that 23% of all graduates entered the teaching profession (see table 4.11). This was one of the lowest percentages among all the colleges, but it was offset by the high number in other professions. By comparison, Gaffield and Marks note than 75% of all Queen's graduates of their group whose careers are known entered teaching, while for University College it is 56%. Gaffield and Marks's catalogue of other professions pursued by their group matches to some extent the list provided by McPherson for other professions (see table 4.12).[31]

WLS/WUA officers chose diverse occupations, but concentrated in teaching and clerical work (see table 4.13). Comparing these figures to those of University College graduates as a whole, the WLS/WUA appears to have provided the bulk of women graduates from University College who entered journalism and the civil service (most of those listed as "clerks" were government clerks). The journalists can most certainly be associated with the organizations' continued focus on the *Varsity* and *Sesame*, and the civil servants connected with their administrative goals of the society. But the WLS/WUA did not seem to encourage its officers to go very much outside the traditional occupational choices for women. Only two were inspired to break their way into the male preserve of the law. One of these, Vera Parsons, received a significant share of the vote for the 1946 bencher elections, but on the whole few other graduates were prepared to follow her.[32] Both of the women who became professors within ten years of their graduation did so in the United States, with one of them (Elizabeth Laird) eventually ending up in the *Canadian Who's Who*, despite the fact that her work in physics was conducted almost entirely south of the border. And only one become a medical doctor, working exclusively as a medical missionary in India.

McPherson's 1920 observation that teaching was the only assured future for women graduates[33] is echoed by almost all who have studied the possible careers for university women. Paula LaPierre asserts that "University College produced the most graduates and the most teachers. Many of the earliest pioneers who had struggled to gain entrance, used their degrees as tickets of entry to the public high school system."[34] Teaching as a career path has been studied in detail by Susan

Gelman and little can be added here that would improve upon her work. What should be highlighted, however, is the peculiar double standard that women faced as high school teachers in the province of Ontario. Gelman paraphrased J.F. MacDonald as noting that "The work of men and women teachers appeared equal, whereas in reality men performed two services and women only one. Men not only served the school board by teaching, they also provided a service to the state by marrying and rearing children. Most women teachers were spinsters and constituted 'practically a celibate teaching order, though not under vows.' They therefore provided only one service, that of teaching."[35] Of course, women were generally not allowed to be teachers while they were married. Female teachers were thus in an inescapable bind.

The other critical point relates to the average careers of female teachers as opposed to male ones. The "leakage" of women out of the profession due to marriage was recognized as a problem at the time. Peter Sandiford of the Faculty of Education at the University of Toronto noted in 1914 that the average professional career of women teachers was 5.85 years, while for men it was 14.2.[36] Some impressionistic data about this leakage as it applied to WLS/WUA officers can be presented. Five years after graduation fifty of them are known to have become high school teachers; eight married during that time. After ten years thirty-nine were still in the profession; seven more of those had married. Twenty years out only twenty-eight teachers remained. Fifteen of the twenty-two who left the profession between five and twenty years after graduating did so because of marriage.

In addition to those women who had careers in teaching that lasted until five years after graduation, there were others who envisaged teaching careers that never materialized. A study of the records of the University of Toronto Faculty of Education from 1908/09 to 1919/20 located twenty-four former officers of the WLS/WUA. Three of them never taught, and one went west to teach. Another taught for only one year before marrying. One in six who began teacher training did not teach (it is not clear whether or not some of these failed the course). Beyond those cases are two others who married four years and three years after graduation respectively. This leakage among WLS/WUA officers cannot be accurately compared with other data from other similar cohorts. Susan Gelman states only "Many of the women secondary school teachers in my study were career teachers, who taught for well over twenty years." Gelman does note that University of Toronto Faculty of Education records indicate that "only" 31 per cent of its graduates married, but does not evaluate Sandiford's claim about differing lengths of teaching careers for women compared with men.[37]

The experience of the WLS/WUA officers appears to show that such concerns about leakage were entirely justified by observable experience. The solution was to allow married women to teach.

WOMEN OF DISTINCTION

Margaret Ray was perplexed by yet another fact she discovered in the course of her research on female university graduates. Just as with the men of the Lit. from 1891 to 1921, those who examined women's post-graduation lives were distressed by their lack of participation in public life. The state had pressed the issue of higher education for women, but women seemed to be doing little in return to enhance the political progress of either Ontario or Canada. In a colloquy in the *University Monthly*, Ray noted that only one in every hundred women graduates had "any great claim to public recognition." To justify her assertion Ray could turn to a long history of women's marginalization:

Have you read "What Every Woman Knows?" How many of the 45% engaged in that most difficult of all partnerships – marriage – get the credit for the share they have contributed to their husband's success? How many men in public life have risen to their present eminence largely through the labour and devotion of some subordinate who is classified in the census as a "female clerk?" And do you realize what it has cost those fifteen women of distinction, to reach the heights they have attained? Have you any conception of the almost insuperable obstacles which beset the paths of women who seek for recognition in the business and professional arena?[38]

All of Ray's points are well taken. The difficulty thus becomes how to evaluate student leadership as preparation for leadership in later life, when the route to positions of authority for women were fraught with more societal obstacles than was the case for men.

Definitions in these instances are difficult. If the definition of a woman of distinction was recognition in the various who's who volumes that include both men and women, then the WLS/WUA facilitated that achievement. Instead of 1 in 100 of female graduates, the rate was 1 in 50, as 4 of the 211 former officers made it into the directories. Three of these women were involved in education. Marion B. Ferguson served a long career as dean of women at University College, Norma H. Ford became a fellow of the Royal Society of Canada through her work in biology, and Elizabeth R. Laird finally merited inclusion when her long expatriate career in the United States landed her a professorial post in physics at the University of Western Ontario. Vida Peene, the fourth of the group, made her mark in cultural activities and ended as an important member of the Canada Council. Of the four, only Ford married.

Biographical dictionaries were not, however, places in which women were found in great numbers. As Robert Lanning notes, "the contribution of women to the settlement and consolidation of Canada was crucial. But their not having a central, determining role – possible only with a recognized base of social power – meant that women did not press upon the public domain in Canada."[39] Henry Morgan's *Types of Canadian Women*, for example, was comprised for the better part by those women who were married to prominent Canadians, meaning that "their short biographies were merely conduits for additional praise for their exemplary husbands."[40] Inclusion in biographical dictionaries is thus too narrow a criterion by which to evaluate the leadership role of women.

If the criteria for evaluation are widened to those who attained leadership positions in political, philanthropic, and benevolent activities, the number of women of distinction who passed through the WLS/WUA rises to 25 of 211, or 12%. This only covers the known cases as reported by the University of Toronto Alumni Association's records. On the surface, this percentage was far lower that the two-thirds that Gaffield and Marks discovered among Queen's alumnae, but they were measuring participation and not leadership.

The variety of leadership among the twenty-five was diverse, but not surprisingly it centred around the University of Toronto. As Paula LaPierre points out, newly-founded university alumnae associations were very much dependant on previous women graduates for their survival. At University College the alumnae association was founded in 1898, and strove to improve facilities for women at the college.[41] Eight former officers of the WLS/WUA attained the presidency of this association. One other became president of the whole University of Toronto Alumni Federation during the Second World War. A detailed search of the minutes of the University College Alumnae Association located twenty-three others (not counted among the twenty-five leaders) who held positions on its executive from 1898 to 1918. To put this in perspective, the actual membership of the Alumnae Association for most of this period never rose above fifty. In 1906/07 the association reported that there were 406 graduates alive, of whom only 53 were members. Of those fifty-three, nineteen were former WLS officers.[42]

In the University Women's Club, which was founded in 1903 at a meeting presided over by former WLS officer and future Alumnae Association president Grace Hunter,[43] former officers of women's organizations at University College could also be found in large numbers.

Seven rose to high positions in this organization, and two – Hunter and Annie Patterson – were sent as delegates to the conferences of the International Federation of University Women. The University leadership positions can be completed by noting that another former officer became secretary of the university Skating Club.

Outside of their alma mater several women attained high positions in women's organizations that had somewhat larger ambitions. Two were prominent in the Women's Canadian Club, one in the Imperial Order of Daughters of the Empire (IODE), and another in the Young Women's Christian Association (YWCA). To mention the YWCA is to blur the lines between employment and volunteer leadership. Several other women worked for the YWCA, including Marion Ferguson before her career at University College began, but they appear to have been paid for their labour, which immediately moves it out of the realm being discussed here. Two other women became presidents of the Women's Missionary Society, although it might be noted that both were married to clergymen. Another former officer served with the Red Cross. A final member of this category would probably be Helen D'Avingnon, who founded the Girl Guides of Windsor and served as its president for eight years.

Leaving aside the one former officer whose philanthropic activities in the United States were mentioned in alumni records but not classified, there remain three cases, all of them in the political sphere. One of these careers appears to have been short-lived, as Margaret Boyle served for one year as secretary of the Women's Liberal Association and then disappeared from the political scene. Two others, however, were active in securing the vote for women and then in making sure it was used. Isabel R. McCurdy served with the Equal Franchise League in Canada from 1910 to 1917, a group that argued for suffrage as "a means of achieving other necessary reforms," while disdaining radical tactics.[44] That McCurdy was serious about the vote is shown by her service as corresponding secretary for the League of Women Voters in Canada from 1923 to 1928. In the United States, Jeannette Atwater Street performed a similar role, using her influence as the wife of Professor Ernest C. Jeffrey to lobby for similar franchise reforms. For her efforts she ended up on the honour roll of the League of Women Voters in the United States.

One area in which the women of the WLS/WUA were not found in large numbers was in missionary and settlement work. Only three became missionaries, and only five are mentioned in the literature on the settlement movement. Vera Parsons was briefly a volunteer resident at the Central Neighbourhood House in Toronto before embarking on her law career, and Alice McLean was on the staff of Evangelia House before her marriage.[45] Mono McLaughlin was a member of the University Settlement Women's Club[46] before starting her work as a factory inspector. Lucy W. Robinson and Fannie Storey both served for one year as volunteers for Central Neighbourhood House.[47] Robinson then married Rev. George P. Bryce and went with him to India as a missionary. A growing body of literature now exists on missionary and settlement work by women in nineteenth-century Canada, especially by university women, but little of it could be connected with the WLS/WUA.[48] From 1908 to 1911 the WLS reported contact with Evangelia House, noting "every day some of the members of the Society t[ook] classes" there, but there was no sense of how many students this engaged.[49]

With the exception of missionary and settlement work, then, the women of the WLS/WUA provided a clear picture of the range of possible avenues to public distinction for female university graduates of this early period. By pursuing these activities, they moved beyond traditional gender roles and surpassed their biographical place. Robert Lanning concludes that in Canada "whether or not women pursued paid labour outside of the home, the household remained their physical and biographical domain"; fidelity, not leadership, was their key characteristic.[50] This domestic norm meant that their work was not adequately recognized at the time.

Disentangling their experience serving on the WLS/WUA from other factors that may have led these women to their chosen volunteer work is difficult. But the general rate of distinction among these former student leaders, given the nature of the society into which they were thrust and the essentially limited roles to which they were for most of this period assigned, cannot be ignored. Indeed, seventy-five years later many of them were named by local chapters of the Canadian Federation of University Women to their official register of "notable women," the story of their lives preserved in the National Archives of Canada.[51]

A SEPARATE SPHERE

Women at University College in the 1891-to-1921 period faced a number of serious dilemmas. They had been admitted to the institution in a spirit of equality, but they were still perceived in many quarters as interlopers. Equal access to university degrees did not mean equal access to courses and certainly did not mean equal access to the extra-curriculum. Under these circumstances, women were forced to define a separate sphere whereby they too could achieve the benefits of activities outside of classes to supplement the lessons they were learning.

However, those who planned extracurricular activities for women were caught on the horns of another dilemma. Although a university education had been quite clearly identified with career training (or, at least, character training) for men, there was no such clear connection for women. Many entered University College with the full knowledge that after graduation they would quickly marry and raise families. Other women had already rejected marriage, and saw no reason not to use their extracurricular activities as a supplement for future public life. These tensions played themselves out in the organization of the WLS. Those women interested in debating were often challenged by those who saw no purpose in it and who preferred to read from Tennyson and play musical instruments. A prolonged battle between "practical" and "ornamental" extracurricular activities was the result.

The same dilemmas faced women after they graduated from university. Career options were limited almost exclusively to teaching. For those who chose to marry, a public career was out of the question and the stark choice between marriage and an occupation outside the home must have been frustrating to some graduates. Those that opted for marriage tended to seek husbands who were university-educated professionals or financially secure businessmen. They then melted into the background, where their contributions to the success of their husbands and any personal achievements of their own went largely unreported and were certainly unheralded.

Former WLS/WUA officers who chose to have public careers were similarly less than praised by those who commented on them. Teachers, especially, were suspected of being prone to marriage at any point, and few of them were given the credit they deserved, even for having long careers. They faced a double standard in that they were prohibited from marriage if they wanted to keep their jobs, yet criticized for not doing their part to raise families. Those few women who achieved national prominence did so against tremendous odds.

Fundamentally, however, what is known about the female graduates of University College for this period is overshadowed by what is not known. Women had achieved a place at university, but they had not entered the consciousness of university administrators or alumni associations. Although future generations of university women depended on alumnae association fundraising in order to sustain building projects, the central record-keepers did not take the same pains to track them as they did for male graduates, nor did they spend devote much space in alumni magazines to praise their contributions to Canadian society. Silently they entered university, silently they moved through academia, and silently they moved on to their future lives. The task of retrieving their stories and placing them in the proper context of Canadian history has, even after a generation of scholarship, just begun.

5 The Administrators: The Lit., 1922–58

The officers of the Lit. in the nineteenth and early twentieth centuries were logical precursors of the professional gentlemen that they would in the fullness of time become. From 1922 to 1958 a new generation of students emerged as managers and businessmen who increasingly found themselves in possession of a university degree.

After 1920 the University of Toronto also transformed, most likely unwittingly, from a national to a local educational institution. This third cohort of officers of the Literary and Athletic Society was largely from the Toronto area. Percentages for all other Ontario places of origin had fallen: southwestern Ontario dropped from 31% to 13%, eastern Ontario from 12% to 5%, and the rest of Ontario from 23% to 10%. Toronto and environs, however, rose from 26% to 52%. These figures are somewhat counterbalanced in the case of the Lit. by the fact that overall Ontario origins dropped from 92% to 81%, as more students from western Canada and the United States became officers of the society (see table 5.1).

University of Toronto authorities were worried by the implications of these trends. As President Sidney Smith reported in 1947/8, "the geographical distribution of students is a matter of concern to us ... we are not serving as we should the gifted high-school students in rural areas."[1] This may have been so, but it is also possible that these students were taking advantage of other educational opportunities closer to their places of origin. Paul Axelrod notes that during the

1930s "Canadian universities in general served primarily local and provincial constituencies," with few students registering in universities distant from their homes.[2] University College, like the larger institution of which it was a part, also followed this pattern.

As far as parental occupation is concerned (table 5.2), sons of farmers declined sharply in number. While in the 1890–1921 period, 25% of the officers of the Lit. came from farm families, only 4% did from the 1922–58 era. The farm population of Ontario was declining at the time, but not as sharply as this. Ian Drummond gives the percentage of Ontarians in agricultural work as 46.3% in 1891, 26.4% in 1921, and 18.6% in 1941.[3]

There are two other sources that provide comparative figures for the University of Toronto and the rest of Canada. In 1927/8, President Robert Falconer presented the initial findings of a study by Professor H.R. Kemp (an ex-officer of the Lit.) on the parental origins of University of Toronto students. His figures cover only one year of students in arts, but they show some rough similarities to the officers of the Lit. (see table 5.3). Falconer could only comment on these figures that "it is obvious that far more students proportionally come from professional homes than from those whose heads are in business."[4] These findings are similar to Axelrod's statistics for the fathers of arts students (table 5.4), except for the high figures for semi- and unskilled workers. Axelrod combines four somewhat different universities in his figures, and either this or a coding system different than Kemp's might account for the differences.

The figures for Lit. officers' religious affiliations (table 5.5) show that the number of Presbyterians remained high, continuing the trend of resistance to the United Church. University College was also the institution of choice for a large number of Jewish students, much higher than the Jewish percentage of the Canadian population as a whole. Axelrod goes into some detail about the prejudices at some Canadian universities against the increasing numbers of Jewish students.[5] Religious prejudice, although camouflaged by polite language, also surfaced in reference to University College. Jewish students were singled out by *Varsity* editor L.J. Ryan as being a separate element at the college in 1930. In 1931, another enterprising editor went further, noting:

The University of Toronto is also made up of four colleges, three of which, St. Michael's, Trinity, and Victoria, are of distinct religious denominations ... The fourth, University College, is not sectarian, but its student body is largely Protestant and Jewish ... University College has practically reached its housing limit, and is now in a very congested state. One solution to this overcrowding would be to form a Jewish College – a separate college, for Jewish students, of the same nature, privileges, rules, and tutorial system as the other colleges.

It is notorious on the Campus that the Jewish students and the Gentile mix to an almost negligible extent. They belong to and meet in the same groups, and clubs, and societies; but cases of friendship are so rare as to excite comment ... the formation of a Jewish College would result both in a certain amount of freedom and scope for individualism that the other sects have and that the Jews have not, and also in a solution of the congestion problem in University College.

At this point, the editor quickly backpedalled from the brink of fascist-sounding antisemitism and declared that in the wake of anti-Jewish activities at Quebec universities, such actions would be "suspect" and seen as a precursor to a removal of all Jews from campus. This aim was explicitly disavowed.[6]

The Jewish presence at University College was a clear fact on the campus, and one that did spark some prejudicial comments, no matter how well intentioned some of them might have been. No overt actions, however, against these students has come to light at the college level. In terms of the male population of the college, when their actions were free (and not restrained by the charters of US Fraternities) they practised a tolerance that at University College was well into its third generation.

Political science and commerce students provided almost 40% of all Lit. officers during the 1922–1958 period. Science students were under-represented, as were members of the general course. The under-representation of moderns and English students can most likely be explained by the fact that most of them were women and thus not eligible to run for office. Classics, a traditionally more mixed discipline, maintained a presence similar to the college numbers as a whole (tables 5.6 and 5.7).

These numbers pose an interesting dilemma when analyzed in terms of the evolution of the Literary and Athletic Society. Was the influence of so many commerce students the reason for the Lit.'s development as an administrative body, or did these students run for the Lit. because it was becoming an administrative body? In a sense the question is insoluble, because the development of the commerce course and the modification of the Lit. happened at essentially the same time. Both, then, were manifestations of a changing climate at the university.

Parental influence still shaped students' course choices. This is most evident among the commerce and the general courses. Of the fifty-nine commerce students twenty-one, or 36%, were the sons of businessmen, and fifteen, or 25%, were the sons of supervisory and clerical workers.

Only nine, or 15%, were sons of professionals. Fifty-three percent of all sons of businessmen were in the commerce or general streams, and this figure rises to 62% for those in supervisory or white-collar families. Sons of professionals, meanwhile, were overwhelmingly found in the honours courses (see table 5.8). As with the students of the second cohort, it appears that the career notions of these Lit. officers were shaped at the outset by the influence of their families.

Tables 5.9 and 5.10 show the career choices for this generation of officers of the Literary and Athletic Society. Over half embarked on careers in the professions. Although the ex-officers did not go into business at the same rate that their fathers did, the influence of a new commercial Canada is clearly evident in these tables. Out of the 254 students alive with known occupations after 10 years, 31%, or 79, remained lawyers, a rate comparable to the 1890–1921 period figure of 26%. Accountants, though, rose from 2% to 6%; in contrast, physicians and journalists dropped from 4% to 1.5%, and academics from 19% to 11%. Most strikingly, the clergy dropped from a total of forty-four, or 14%, to a total of four, or 1.5%. Emerging out of nowhere were three "consultants," a new professional category.

Also interesting in the occupational data are the large number who began in white-collar occupations. Five years after graduation, 13% were white-collar workers, as opposed to 4.0% for the 1890–1921 period. Thirty years after graduation, however these white-collar workers declined to 2%. A university education, while apparently not suitable for immediate high-level employment, allowed these graduates to climb rapidly up the business and civil service ladders. In other cases, a shift into a profession occurred, as from the civil service into law, or from business into accountancy.

Geographically, Toronto dominated as graduates' destination of choice. While between 25% and 35% of the previous generation remained in Toronto, the rate rose to 60% for the 1922–58 group. The cumulative percentages of those staying in Ontario rose from 58% to 82%. This cohort moved the least from its places of origin than did any previous group. They were born in Toronto (or Ontario), educated in Toronto, and made their careers in Toronto (or Ontario). While 12% of the 1890–1921 group emigrated to the United States, only 4% to 5% of this group did so. And their immobility could not be shaken by a world war either. While 10% of the previous generation were in Britain or Flanders five years after graduation, only 6% of this group found themselves in the same position. This may be the reason that the death rate for this group was far lower than for the 1890–1921 cohort.

The University of Toronto, then, was not serving as a national institution during the 1922–58 period in the same way that it had in earlier times. Some of this localization was no doubt the result of uncertainty caused by a period of economic depression and global war, which made the risks of long-distance travel more plain. More of it was caused by the growth of Toronto as a business and administrative centre for Canada as a whole, as well as the site of a growing provincial civil service and ever-expanding university in the years after 1945. If jobs for university graduates existed in Toronto, there is little reason to expect that they would have sought them elsewhere. There was no new frontier to conquer that was desperately short of trained personnel, despite one student's advice to his colleagues that these existed "up north, and ... in South America."[7]

THE LAW AND PUBLIC DISTINCTION

The practice of law was still a major career path for Literary and Athletic Society members after graduation, and also still the main route to political participation. Although the participation of these students in actual political campaigning was at its lowest level ever (27 of 318, or 8.4%), only 4 (3 academics and a civil servant) who made a run at office from this group were not lawyers. Of the eleven who sat in provincial or dominion parliaments, eight were lawyers, the exceptions being academics Lloyd Francis and Ralph Loffmark, and civil servant John Moody Roberts. Seven of these eleven became cabinet ministers, three in Ottawa, three in Toronto, and one (Loffmark) in Victoria. By far the most successful of these was William Grenville Davis, premier of Ontario and member of parliament for nearly thirty years. His record was challenged only by Robert Kaplan, who served a similar period as a member of the House of Commons. Those who served politically in this period enjoyed longer careers in politics than did many of the Lit. officers from the previous "political animals" period.

Political office was far from the only career path available to lawyers from the 1922–58 group. But those who did take the political route were saved from the vicissitudes of a profession that was changing more radically than ever before. This generation of lawyers was trained during the stormiest period in the history of legal education in the province of Ontario. A "fierce debate" pitted traditional exponents of apprentice training against those who believed in academic law. Although lawyers in general still believed that a sound liberal education was a useful prelude to a law career, this was always tempered by the practical needs of the profession.[8] Given the uncertainty that surrounded the Law Society's changing decisions, it was not surprising that many prospective lawyers stayed in university for the complete four-year period. They also kept themselves informed about changes that might affect them. In 1952, Albert Strauss, in his introduction for Dean Cecil Wright of the University of Toronto Law School, spoke of University College as a legal "breeding ground" and mentioned the Osgoode Hall-Law School controversy. Dean Wright then spoke on "Legal Education in Ontario." The timing of Wright's speech was not accidental, as Strauss explained to the *Varsity* that the main benefit would be to "all students contemplating going into law, especially those on their final years because he can give us an understanding of the respective position of the University Law School and Osgoode Hall."[9] As always, the Lit. was looking out for the professional interests of its law school-bound members.

This focus on the professional interests of lawyers was not without an effect. Ninety-eight of the 318 ex-officers of the Lit. (31%) had at one point in their lives a foot in the legal profession, even if fewer than that spent their entire careers in it. The group resembled the lawyers of the earliest period in Lit. history. It produced people who had an interest in the academic side of law, including Bora Laskin and Martin Friedland, both of whom were attached to the Faculty of Law at the University of Toronto. As well, eight of the ninety-eight (8%) became benchers of the Law Society, a higher percentage than in the 1890–1921 period. And three of the benchers were active in 1957 when the decision was made to allow university LLB programs to provide entrance to the profession. Just as the Lit. ex-officers of 1854–90 had been connected with a reform in legal education, so too was this group.

As well, a higher percentage became judges.[10] While only 13% of the previous period's lawyers rose to the bench, 21% (twenty-one of ninety-eight) did so in this period. Nineteen of these served as judges in Ontario, one in Manitoba, and one in Alberta, reinforcing again the localized nature of this generation of graduates. Among them were Bora Laskin, chief justice of the Supreme Court of Canada; George Gale, chief justice of Ontario; and Charles Dubin, chief justice of the Court of Appeals. These three do not exhaust the complete list of those serving on superior courts; Joseph Potts and Samuel Grange would also be on such a list. In all senses, then, this was a group of lawyers who moved back into the centre of professional leadership.

There remained a contingent of nine who became businessmen; this figure, however, excluded a large number who were directors of corporations and presidents of companies by virtue of their personal investments. Beverley Matthews, for example, held a considerable number of such positions but still insisted on listing himself as a "lawyer" in the *Canadian Who's Who*. Seven entered the civil service, and two worked for the Toronto Transit Commission. The law also continued to attract those from other areas, as four came to it after careers as an accountant, professor, civil service officer, and journalist respectively. And one left law to become an accountant, thus placing into personal context the conflict between the law and accountancy over jurisdictions such as tax law in post-war Ontario.[11]

Even though new professions were challenging the supremacy of the law, the general outlook for lawyers from the 1922–59 cohort was good. Even in the midst of the Depression, most lawyers could maintain a middle-class status, or, as Moore puts it, "hope to have a car, perhaps to employ a maid, and to secure the education of their children."[12] After the war economic growth, plus an increase in state regulation and public administration, created a need for even more expansion of the legal profession. It also ushered in the era of law firm management in the 1950s and 1960s, with a new emphasis on strategic planning and senior partners. Here one ex-officer of the Lit., Beverley Matthews at McCarthy's, was an acknowledged master.[13]

Evidence of leadership in any other sense remains slight. Robert Carley's influence in the Peterborough Rotary Club or Matthews's role as president of the Toronto Board of Trade fall into the category of anecdotal information and cannot be used analytically. Twenty-seven of the ninety-eight ended up in the *Canadian Who's Who*, and a further two attained listings in the less long-lived *Who's Who in Canadian Law*. These attainments show yet again the connection between legal careers and national prominence. This focus on national prominence, however, obscures the existence of other routes to leadership in society, of which a prime example is James W. Graham's career. Graham was born in Weyburn, Saskatchewan, attended the University of Toronto, was elected to the Lit., received his degree, and returned to Weyburn to have a long legal career, which outside of that small city attracted little notice. In his own way, however, Graham was continuing a pattern that Stewart Wallace had detected many years earlier, and that was still open to university students for whom Toronto had no great lure.

ACCOUNTANCY

Although accountancy had been establishing itself as a profession in Ontario since the 1890s, it was only after the First World War that it began to seek the educational grounding that other professions had insisted on much earlier. The Institute of Chartered Accountants of Ontario (ICAO) took the lead in this regard, out of fear it would lose its primacy in the province. The rigorous standards of the ICAO led ill-trained students to fail their exams, and then to form their own

accountancy associations with looser rules. This was against the interests of the ICAO, which began to look elsewhere than private business
schools for institutions that could educate accountants. The ICAO
decided on Queen's University, which was developing a Commerce
program, and by 1921 Queen's had a four-year program that was
approved by the association.[14] Accountancy, then, was assisting in the
rise of commerce programs in Ontario, which were educating a large
number of students between the wars.[15]

Tension existed in accountancy, just as in law, between education and
training. The poor preparation of most accountants was a matter of
concern for the ICAO, especially during World War II when many qual-
ified accountants enlisted in the armed forces and were unable to train
new students. During this period, certain accounting firms such as Clarkson, Gordon, and Company made training a serious internal matter.[16]
The universities, however, continued to turn out commerce graduates
who became chartered accountants with relative ease. Recognizing these
developments, the ICAO took small steps to encourage students, such as
offering two $1,000 scholarships at the University of Toronto for pro-
spective accountants[17] and occasionally visiting the campus to trumpet
the advantages of accountancy as a career.[18] These developments led the
ICAO to propose in the late 1950s that all prospective CAs hold a university degree. Although there was some difficulty in convincing the universities to change their curricula to suit the needs of accountancy, the
ICAO pressed on with its "1970 proposal" by which every CA in Canada
would have a university degree by that year. This proposal was finally
passed as the "1972 proposal" in 1969, although it drove many
prospective students into other branches of accountancy.[19]

It is thus not surprising that eighteen of the fifty-nine commerce
students who served as officers on the Lit. in this period turned to
chartered accountancy as a profession. There was a growing need for
accountants in Ontario, and except for three who went to British
Columbia, all the graduates stayed in that province. Two did not
remain in the profession for long, one switching to law and the other
to academia and later politics (Ralph Loffmark). Four used accounting
as a route up the business ladder and ended their careers as vice-presidents
or presidents of corporations, the most prominent perhaps being Earl
Orser, the president of London Life. A further two became municipal
accountants in Toronto and Sault Ste. Marie respectively. Accountancy,
like law, was a profession that could lead in different directions.

Unlike law, however, accountancy tended to cluster around specific
companies. Among the eighteen graduates, five spent time with Clarkson,
Gordon, and Company,[20] a phenomenon unknown to the lawyers of
the same period. There is no evidence that Clarkson, Gordon, and

Company deliberately targeted graduates of the University of Toronto, therefore this clustering was most likely connected to the company's stature in the industry and its numerous branches across the country.

Similar to the law, accountancy had extensive internal discipline procedures. Two of the former Lit. officers who entered the profession were caught engaging in improper conduct. One paid a fine and recanted, the other refused and was expelled from the ICAO. Conversely, five of the chartered accountants received entries in the *Canadian Who's Who*; however, four were listed because of their later careers in business and finance, and one (Loffmark) for his political career. Although accountancy had achieved a recognized place in Canadian society and education by the 1922–59 period, accountants themselves were not acknowledged as leaders in society.

LIFE INSURANCE

Life insurance agents, like accountants, struggled in this period with educational requirements and the possibilities of university training. Such ideas had been absent from the profession when the Life Underwriters Association of Toronto was formed in 1906. Although they held their first meeting in Convocation Hall,[21] this seems to have been a matter of finding sufficient space rather than any assumption of shared interest between life insurance agents and higher education. By the 1920s, however, the newly incorporated Life Underwriters Association of Canada (LUAC) had begun negotiations with several universities to provide courses that would be useful for prospective agents. They were able to persuade the University of Toronto to introduce a course of extension lectures in this area in 1925. The lectures, however, dwelt to a great extent on abstract mathematics and not enough on practical problems, which led to poor attendance and a negligible completion rate among those who began the course. In the wake of this setback, extensive negotiations took place between the LUAC and the universities that led the latter to conclude that "the function of the university was to provide a general education. They [the universities] were inclined to the view that the only way to raise the standards of life underwriters was to recruit graduates from the universities and refuse admission to those with lesser educational background."[22] This was further than the LUAC was prepared to go in 1925.

The depression of the 1930s, however, hit the life insurance industry hard, and led those in the field to adopt the LUAC's suggestions that "a smaller, more compact, better selected, better educated, and better trained agency force" was needed in Canada.[23] The LUAC thus was encouraged to put pressure again on the University of Toronto, which reinstated extension courses in life insurance in 1932. These remained optional until 1951, when they became compulsory for all candidates seeking to be registered as certified life underwriters.[24]

For almost this entire period, then, the insurance business maintained a presence on campus. Fifteen of the ex-officers of the Lit. reacted by pursuing careers with insurance companies; for all but one, who went into fire insurance, life insurance was the line of choice. Three did not continue for very long in the business, one quitting to go to law school, another to be a salesman, and the third to join a bond and investment company. Like accountancy, there was a tendency to cluster around specific companies, with three joining Sun Life and two at each of Manufacturer's, Mutual Life, and Excelsior.

These university-trained insurance practitioners also took an interest in the development of their profession and participated in various support organizations. Both Thomas Jarvis and Walter Arnold served as presidents of the Toronto Life Underwriters Association; Harrington Guy was president of the Canadian Life Insurance Officers Association; and George Wallace served on various committees of the Canadian Institute of Actuaries and also organized the curling team for the Toronto Actuaries Club. Two others were able to gain recognition in the *Canadian Who's Who*. Graham Brown was cited for his role in personnel recruitment at Sun Life, and Earl Orser for his presidency at London Life. The move from student leadership to the administration of the life insurance industry was not difficult for these ex-officers of the Literary and Athletic Society.

MEDIA CAREERS

The transition was also easy in the media. Paul Axelrod has noted the extent to which students of the 1930s were exposed to media of various kinds. Student newspapers and yearbooks carried many advertisements, students were frequent patrons of movies from both Hollywood and elsewhere, and they also listened to radio.[25] These predilections became stronger as time went by. In 1951 the University College Parliamentary Club spent a session discussing the possibilities and problems of television, the debate subject being "that in the interests of Canadian culture Television be put completely in the hands of private enterprise."[26]

Although the Lit. did produce the University College *Follies* for the entire period, there was no direct sense that this was preparation for a future career in the entertainment industry. Similarly, experiments with radio debates and production at the University of Toronto seemed to be just that – experiments, or, if not that, simply hobbies. The Lit. would from time to time invite a prominent Canadian journalist to address its meetings. Peter McArthur informed it in 1922 that "Canada offers great opportunities to authors."[27] P.W. Richards, the financial editor of *Saturday Night*, also made an appearance at a meeting in 1937 to discuss future economic systems, and CBC broadcaster Wilson Woodside came in 1940 to discuss current events.[28] Napier Moore, a former editor of *Maclean's*, regaled the Lit. in 1950 with excerpts from "A Pressman's Notebook."[29] These sporadic contacts, and the traditional student press with its tenuous link to the city's journalistic establishment, were the only connections between University College and the media.

The fact remains, however, that 29 of the 318 ex-officers of the Lit. from this period pursued media-related careers. These careers were far more complex than the pursuits of lawyers or accountants. They break down, however, into five general groups: print journalists; filmmakers; television personalities; advertisers; and publishers.

Of the five areas, print journalism had the longest tradition of employing university graduates. References have been made earlier in this study to careers that former Lit. officers from previous generations made for themselves in the world of newspaper journalism. Ten from the 1922–58 period began in this area, but only four made any long-term commitment to the profession. The other six quit, though three of them stayed in the media industry as, respectively, a public relations consultant, a publisher, and the chair of the Canadian Newsprint Association. The other three left the world of media entirely, one to become a lawyer, one to take over his father's clothing business, and the other to become deputy minister of labour for Ontario. Unfortunately, there is no general survey available for most media developments in Canada, and the lack of staying power of these print journalists cannot be explained.

Three of the twenty-nine former officers became involved with the motion picture industry. One of these, George W. Peters, was in the management end of things as secretary for University Films; he eventually quit that job to take up public relations for Pacific Petroleum in Calgary. The other two were filmmakers. David Bairstow and Tom Daly each had careers of over thirty years with the National Film Board of Canada (NFB), with Daly being reckoned as "one of the most significant creative figures at the NFB."[30] The three who became involved with television are just as well known. E. Ross McLean's career with the CBC was cut short by an early death, but both Patrick Watson and Harry Rasky are still active in the television industry. Watson is most famous for his work with the controversial CBC public affairs program *This Hour has Seven Days*, and Rasky for his biographical *Raskymentaries* of famous people.[31] In his biography of Tom

Daly, D.B. Jones notes that John Grierson of the NFB simultaneously "valued intellect and formal education", but he also preferred "knowledge that was practical, useful, [and] applicable in a complex industrial society." Grierson nonetheless informed Stuart Legg that Daly was "Bright. University. Teacher manque. Should be our kind. Brutalise him in the usual way."[32] Untrained by their university courses, ex-officers of the Lit. required "brutalisation," it seems, to perform adequately in the world of film and television.

The eight who went into advertising were only slightly better prepared. The Literary and Athletic Society had in the 1920s engaged Osgoode Hall in a debate on the topic "Resolved that, in advertising appeals, style should be emphasized above value," with Osgoode successfully upholding the value of style.[33] Certainly, those involved with the activities of the Lit. had to see that they were well advertised, but this does not seem to have been enough preparation on which to lay a foundation for a career in the business. Stephenson and McNaught's chatty 1940 study, *The Story of Advertising in Canada*, does make one slight allusion to the need for education as a pre-requisite for effective members of the industry. At the end of the section entitled "The Canadian Market," Stephenson and McNaught state, "Enough has been said to indicate that the nature of the Canadian market makes necessary a detailed knowledge of its constituents and reactions if advertising appeals are to be fully effective." The two claim that this knowledge can only be fully acquired by someone "who has … had the long and intimate acquaintance with the Canadian people which is possible only for one who is himself a Canadian."[34] Clearly there was a need for intelligent Canadians to create advertisements in Canada, and a university degree was thus not a liability for those considering an advertising career. Four of the eight, however, found advertising to be less than challenging. Three of these stayed connected to their original intentions, one becoming the manager of the magazines division of Maclean Hunter, one a management consultant, and the third the president of Canada Dry. The only one of the eight to quit his original media career did so to become a social worker. This left the five who went into publishing, all but one of whom remained in that business. The lone exception, Garrick Clarke, made a startling career move from publishing to the pulpit of the United Church of Canada.

The twenty-nine intertwined media careers, disconnected as they were from the traditional goals of the university, and distant from any new ideals that the universities pursued during the 1922–58 period, are interesting examples of how the outside environment could influence the future paths of university graduates. Eight of these men ended up in the *Canadian Who's Who*, but not always as a result of their media careers. Thomas Eberlee was better known as a civil servant, Douglas Gowdy as a businessman, and John A. Lowden as a management consultant. The only man among this group to land in the *Canadian Who's Who* as a result of his advertising career was George MacDonell of Canadian General Electric. Ian Montagnes was noted as a publisher and Charles Vining as the chair of the Newsprint Association; that left only Harry Rasky and Patrick Watson to be recognized as journalists of national distinction. This list, of course, omits University College's two most famous media figures. Although both Frank Schuster and Johnny Wayne were prominent in the casts of the University College *Follies*, neither was able to take much time away from the honing of their act to run for, let alone win, an election at the Literary and Athletic Society. Instead, they used their time at the college to work on their individual pursuits, achieving, in time, remarkable international success.

CAREERS IN EDUCATION

Perhaps the weakest claim that the Lit. was somehow instilling a primarily managerial ethic in its officers was that which can be made for the thirty-six who ended up in education. Although it is true that expanding enrolment after World War II required that professors deal with larger classes and thus learn new skills, this was hardly the same sort of management issue that a lawyer or accountant had to face. These thirty-six former officers can be seen more as having followed a traditional post-university career path that was unshaken by any Lit. activities.

By this point in Canadian history, the divide between university and high school teaching was nearly complete. Twenty-nine of the thirty-six spent their careers as university professors, twelve of them at the University of Toronto. The influence of the United States as a possible work location had diminished, with only six leaving Canada. The rest spread beyond Toronto to the rest of Canada, with two ending up in Halifax and two in Waterloo, new destinations for ex-Lit. officers. Only two became university presidents, Donald Campbell at the University of Manitoba and Donald Forster at the University of Guelph. An additional five became deans. Clearly, this cadre did not include the same quota of academic administrative leaders as the 1890–1921 group had produced.

All seven of the high school teachers found work in Ontario. Three of these became principals or vice-principals of schools, one moved up to become director of business education, and one rose to become dean of the Ontario College of Education. Strangely, though, in this period one other ex-officer of the Lit. became a principal of an elementary school, a position for which he was completely overqualified.

Education in this period proved to be a stable occupation as far as this group was concerned. Only one quit the profession, moving from an assistant professorship into the law. Two others, however, moved from the clergy into education, one actually remaining in the church and teaching at the University of Toronto and the other quitting to teach high school in Mississauga. Thirteen of the thirty-six ended up in who's who volumes, twelve in Canada and one in the United States; they were all professors.

CIVIL SERVANTS

The 1922–58 period saw an expansion in the number of ex-officers of the Lit. who took civil service positions. Leaving aside those who worked as civil servants in wartime with institutions such as the Wartimes Prices and Trades Board and the War Information Bureau, thirteen former Lit. officers entered the civil service. The aforementioned Thomas Eberlee and Kenneth Hignell (of the Ontario Department of Transport) served as provincial bureaucrats. Eleven others worked in the Canadian public service in Ottawa. These Ottawa men differed from their predecessors; they were not the doctor-coroners of an earlier era. Instead of being simply transformed into government bureaucrats by an expanding state, they were professional civil servants.

Six of them pursued careers as diplomats with the Department of External Affairs – this was an avenue virtually untravelled before 1922. In the aftermath of the First World War, however, Canada began to have a foreign policy that could be distinguished, however slightly, from that of the British Empire. A need for Canadians to fill these posts grew, and in the era following the establishment of the United Nations in 1945 it expanded significantly. It was into this climate that Saul Rae and Paul Bridle, among others, graduated and found their niches.[35] The other five joined various other departments in Ottawa.

These eleven men entered a civil service that had changed significantly since the earlier period, especially in Ottawa. Serious reforms to the system of recruiting civil servants had eliminated to a great extent political patronage as a factor influencing employment. Competitive civil service exams became a reality after 1918.[36] One chairman of the Civil Service Commission, C.H. Bland, even went so far as to state in 1945 that the government had made a concrete effort to "secure the best minds among university graduates" for the civil service, "the emphasis being placed on quality, adaptability, and promise of development rather than on specific knowledge in any particular field."[37] This impulse from the centre dovetailed nicely with the emergence of the Lit. as an organization stressing administrative competence in many fields of endeavour.

The civil service was thus able to tempt one university-trained journalist and one university-trained Chrysler dealer out of their jobs and into public affairs. But there was no guarantee that university-educated men would find public service to their liking. Four of the civil servants who went to Ottawa left for other careers, one in employee relations at Imperial Oil, another to the law, and a third to academia. The fourth, John Moody Roberts, made the leap from the civil service to the House of Commons. Only two civil servants were noted from this group in the who's who volumes. Thomas Eberlee has already been mentioned, and the other was Ronald A. Gould, assistant chief electoral officer for Canada.

TRADITION AND INNOVATION

Paul Axelrod has noted the tensions in the university system during the 1930s between "proponents of intellectual depth on the one hand and advocates of serviceable schooling on the other."[38] This tension led to the creation of new courses such as those in commerce, and attempts to connect with the business community in order to better prepare graduates for the realities of a changing Canada. Axelrod has noted a prejudice against university men among business leaders in Canada, who "continued to place a great premium on the value of having employees – whatever their educational backgrounds – work their way up through corporate ranks from positions of minimal status."[39]

This custom began to change as time went on, and certain business professions, such as accountancy, life insurance, and advertising, began to recognize the advantages of university-trained practitioners. Sons businessmen were being sent to university to take commerce courses to prepare themselves for business life. Even in such professions as the law, a culture of management was developing that made experience with these issues a useful preparation for later career development.

Certainly, the choice of careers in later life made by this cohort of Lit. officers increasingly encompassed management and administration. There were exceptions, of course, such as the academic contingent and the journalists. In these cases the traditional role of the university as a transmitter of knowledge to those who would be responsible for passing this wisdom on to later generations could not be challenged by any student society.

Tradition was, though, tempered by innovation. The university continued to supply graduates for new enterprises, such as the television and film industries, and for the new concerns of Canadian society, such as foreign affairs. Far from giving entree to a closed group of lawyers, clergy, and teachers, by 1959 there was a bewildering array of occupations open to the individualists that University College was producing.

Many of the ex-officers of the Lit. in this period were able to go on to impressive careers in politics and law. Others became active professional leaders in the worlds of accountancy and insurance sales. Some, however, remained outright failures; among them were yet another disbarred lawyer and the first defrocked (and deflocked) clergyman. There was also a smattering of those who began their careers on the bottom of the business ladder and never managed to climb up. As the Lit. moved into its second century, its role in leadership training seemed to have less relevance, having been supplanted by a focus on management and administrative skills that, just like the obsession with "public men" in the 1890–1921 period, was an accurate reflection of the society – and the college – to which it belonged.

6 Fighting for a Place: The Women's Undergraduate Association, 1922–58

The men and women at University College had been closing the gaps between themselves since the 1920s, moving increasingly toward a common extracurricular experience. These converging paths can also be extended back to their origins, if not so much forward to their future careers. In terms of place of birth, for example, the same general patterns apply. Although more women (on the WUA) than men (on the Lit.) were born outside of the Toronto environs (50% vs. 48%), the figures for Ontario are identical, and the students' origins elsewhere in Canada are also roughly the same (see table 6.1). There is no sense that the University of Toronto was less of a local organization for either men or women. Lee Stewart has noted that the University of British Columbia (UBC) in this period exhibited similar demographic trends. Between 79% and 87% of UBC co-eds came from Canada, but only 60% from British Columbia.[1]

Greater divergence from the men can be found among the parental origins of the WUA officers (table 6.2). Compared to 32% for the Lit. officers, 45% of the WUA executive had fathers in professional occupations, and there were also a few more whose fathers were in supervisory occupations. The percentages for farmers, however, are identical. This to some extent confounds any simple economic explanation for the difference between the professional occupation rates. For times of depression and war, the general assumption is that women who attended university came from families that were better off than the men's because education for women was discretionary while for men it was necessary.[2] In the case of artisanal and white-collar families, this appears to have been true for the WUA and the Lit. during the 1922–58 period; however, the similarity of the farm figures and the low numbers of businessmen makes this generalization hard to support. Stewart's comparative figures for UBC do not help in this instance. While she gives figures of between 22% and 33% for professional origins and between 23% and 27% for business origins for female students in various years between 1929/30 and 1949/50, she also includes a large number of "private means" students, which my study was not designed to locate and that may undermine significantly the possibility of comparison.[3]

Many professionals during this period accepted that higher education for women was desirable. Among the fathers of the WUA officers were eleven accountants, auditors, or actuaries; nineteen educators; eleven clergymen; twenty-six legal professionals; twelve dentists; seventeen engineers; and thirty-six medical men. The business fathers were equally diverse, from druggists and hardware merchants to the presidents of automobile and life insurance companies. Stewart makes the point that in the 1920s "neither the university nor popular opinion could fully accept that a university degree for a woman, given her destiny to marry and become a homemaker, might be necessary or worthwhile as for a man."[4] Enough information about higher education for women was nonetheless circulating; all fathers had the opportunity to send their daughters to university, and increasingly they were doing so.

The available data on the religious backgrounds of the 342 WUA officers from 1922 to 1958 also show significant divergences from that for the men of the same period. Many more were found in the protestant denominations, especially among the Anglicans. The reason for this was the relative absence of Roman Catholic and especially Jewish women among the ranks of the WUA officers (see table 6.3).

WOMEN'S SUBJECTS

Although there is evidence that the extracurricular activities of men and women were drawing closer together, and that therefore the separate sphere meant less and less, in some critical ways it was just as solid a concept as ever. A.B. McKillop quotes a Queen's student in 1928 as declaring "What are the non-compulsory classes that are attended by men? Natural science, math, economics, etc., are largely filled with them. Language and history are regarded as women's subjects and it is a brave or foolish male who majors in these."[5] With the possible exception of history, these divisions held true at University College. The percentage of WUA officers coming from the general stream was larger than for the men (see table 6.4). Among the honours programs, a far greater percentage of women chose sociology, psychology, English, and modern languages, and a substantial group was still to be found in household science. Nothing should be made of the gender differences for students in physical and health education, because the WUA allowed an ex-officio spot for those students on its executive for ten years, while the men never did. Even taking into account this exception, however, the separation of men's and women's fields was clearly delineated.

There were, though, signs of change during the era under scrutiny. Seven women majoring in political science, sixteen in history, and six in commerce pointed to the possibilities available for female students. Although these women represented a tiny fraction of the total enrolment at the University of Toronto, they established beachheads on which many other women would land in years to come.

WOMEN'S CAREERS

The amount of data on careers of the 342 ex-officers of the WUA, as opposed to their course choices, is disappointingly sparse. Available alumnae information after 1945 is poor, and many of the questionnaires I sent to those for whom an address could be found were not returned. Conclusions about the careers of university women in this period were thus more difficult to formulate than those regarding their origins, which were better documented in the university's records.

In terms of geography, there is every reason to believe that as many of the former WUA leaders stayed in Toronto as did the ex-officers of the Lit. – the character of University College as a local institution evidently applied equally to women. As far as careers are concerned, only a few joined the business world. The media appears to have been the entry point for these women, who largely became advertisers and publishers. In one case, a graduate went on to own a tea shop in New York City. The others who did not marry followed to a large extent the employment patterns established in an earlier era. The known professional occupations of those graduates after five years – which did not change much over the following years – are forty-eight educators, five journalists, four librarians, four psychologists, four scientists, three social workers, three nurses, two physicians, and two lawyers.

The large number in education should not come as a surprise. Twenty-seven of them taught in high schools, four in secondary schools, and two in elementary schools. Perhaps seven were employed in universities five years after graduation;[6] and this figure rose to a dozen twenty years out, most holding the junior ranks of lecturer and assistant professor. There is a clear dichotomy between the number of women who were trained to be university professors and those who were able to find such work. Fifty-eight of the 342 ex-officers of the WUA in this cohort are known to have attained degrees higher than a BA, a greater percentage than in the period before or after (see table 6.7). Of the fifty-eight, forty-seven married. Although the opening of graduate school programs to women may have seemed like a step forward, in fact in many cases progress was an illusion. The possibilities for advancement for a woman with an MA, given the hiring practices of the universities, were still slim.[7] As Donald Wright points out, "if a woman was encouraged to do graduate work, and if she did find a supportive advisor, she encountered almost universal discrimination at the next level: the labour market. Here her sex proved an all but insurmountable barrier precisely because she could not abandon her sex ... It was an indelible marker of difference that set her apart from her male counterparts."[8]

For the other professions, the lack of data available makes it hard to draw any conclusions. Christopher Moore points out that only a "handful" of women were called to the bar between the 1940s and the 1960s, and that only between 1969 and 1973 did numbers begin to rise.[9] For social work, Sara Z. Burke has addressed the struggle the University of Toronto went through trying to transform the image of its department from "a young ladies' finishing school" to a legitimate source of professional training.[10] The occupational choices for women graduating in this period had not changed as drastically as they had for their male counterparts.[11]

MARRIAGE VS. PUBLIC CAREER

Marriage remained a common experience for university-educated women. Twenty-three (7%) never married, and marital status is unknown for another thirty-one (9%). This leaves a marriage rate of 84% (288 of 342) for the group as a whole. Vernoica Strong-Boag lists slightly higher figures for Canadian women as a whole, with approximately 89% of all women married by the age of 49 in 1921, 1931, and 1941.[12] Of the spouses, 111 were university graduates, and another 59 belonged to professions for which a university degree or some form of higher training was necessary. This meant that over 50% of the married university-educated women had husbands who were similarly educated. The real figure is no doubt larger, as the occupations of only 221 of the 288 spouses have been identified.

Among the husbands were thirty-two in the legal profession, twenty-one academics, thirty medical men, fifteen engineers, thirteen accountants/auditors/actuaries, nine salesmen, four life insurance agents, four dentists, and three diplomats, along with a variety of businessmen, consultants, and managers. Fourteen were known solely by their military ranks. There is no sense that these women were following a pattern that can be isolated and explained simply by their choice of husbands, although there is a seemingly middle-class bent to many. Only thirty-five of the spouses are known to have attended University College, and of those six were officers of the Literary and Athletic Society, showing that the joint activities of the two organizations did not have a striking effect on the marriage patterns of the WUA officers.

Most of those who married did so shortly after graduation, but a few waited some time before making that decision. The average age of marriage was very close to the Canadian average, which fluctuated between twenty-three and twenty-five between 1921 and 1941.[13] The 288 married women produced 536 known children, an average of 1.8 (table 6.8). Emily Nett gives the fertility rate for all women in Canada at this time as between 2.5 and 3.5 children.[14] The gaps in alumnae data, however, make the figure of 1.8 for these women doubtful as an actual average, and there is a chance that the true figure is closer to the Canadian norm.[15]

Female university graduates still had a difficult decision to make: whether to get married or to have a career. The inappropriateness of combining the two for the first generations of university women was socially ingrained. As Strong-Boag puts it, "Since traditional views of marriage did not easily encompass female independence, many Canadians, particularly men, found it difficult to accept the idea of so-called working wives."[16] Even into the 1950s, after a brief period of liberation during the Second World War, the cult of domesticity remained strong in Canada, leading to an emphasis on women remaining in the home.[17]

However, just as women and men on the university campus were coming closer together in terms of their extracurricular pursuits, they were also drawing together in the belief that combining marriage and a career was possible. Among this cohort of former WUA officers, forty were able to combine the two roles. Thirty of these, to be sure, graduated after 1945, but even in the period before World War II the concept of the working mother had begun to take hold in the minds of the female students of University College.

The ten ex-officers who graduated before 1945 and pursued careers in tandem with marriage largely did so either as extensions of traditional gender roles, or outside of Canada. Three became professors –

in Los Angeles, Washington State, and Wisconsin. Of the remaining seven, one was a music consultant, another a director of family life education, and yet another a panellist on a CBC television show directed at consumers. This left a liaison officer for the International Council of Women at the United Nations, a secretary, a public relations consultant (in New York State), and two high school teachers. Only the last two represented something rather different, the married high school teacher being an unusual creature in Ontario at the time.

Those who graduated after 1945 pursued somewhat more diverse careers. Education, though, continued to be highly popular. Six of the post-1945 graduates became professors (all of them in Canada), and another seven were teachers. In four of these cases, it seems that they taught in their homes – two were piano instructors, and the other two identified themselves as teacher/housewife. Educational politics, however, was also an issue for the married woman, and two of them became "chairmen" (the gendered term was still current) of school boards. The two researcher/writers and two consultants among the twenty-nine may also have strayed from the home. Certainly, the two social workers, lawyer, psychologist, therapist, and nutritionist entered professions that put them in the public eye as married career women.

In the absence of clear statistics on the issue, the figure of over 10% of former WUA officers who combined marriage and a career can only be regarded as high for the period. Given the media attention paid to women who went from university straight to the home and stayed there, the fact that so many among this group did not do so is impressive. Indeed, it is another clear indication of the convergence of male and female university students between 1922 and 1959.

McKillop comments that after 1951 "women continued to struggle for an equal place on both sides of the lectern. The search of women for their rightful place within the academic community ... became the main symbol of a larger hope for democracy and justice in academic life."[18] Alison Prentice and colleagues add, "The ideal of equal opportunity for the sexes that had been so widely touted during the war became a dominant theme in post-war education ... Full equality, however, remained an elusive goal."[19] The struggle to achieve that objective unfolded under seemingly impossible conditions. Even progressive thinkers such as Frank Underhill did not think women deserved the same treatment in the academy as men, and he openly doubted that any of his female students were truly interested in their work.[20] Women continued to be the object of derision in the student press, and were still considered to lie outside the pale of "fellowship" that admission to Hart House provided to male students.

THE END OF THE SEPARATE SPHERE

It was only natural that women would react to such prejudice, and they did so at almost every Canadian university. At Queen's female students formed Levana, a society that in the 1920s acted "almost like an independent faculty within the university."[21] At McGill they were represented by the Women Students' Union, because women at that university were prevented by the constitution of the McGill Students' Society from exercising representation in proportion to their actual enrolment.[22] The Women's Undergraduate Association at University College followed this pattern, defining, as we have seen, a separate sphere within the university.

By the end of the 1950s, however, many aspects of this segregation seemed antiquated. Women's enrolment in post-secondary institutions continued to rise, and their numbers alone gave them a certain degree of clout within those institutions, especially in terms of finances. When women were finally granted access to the McGill Students' Union in the 1940s, it was because their compulsory fees were needed to help balance the account books of the formerly all-male organization.[23] At the University of Toronto, women had been given equal representation on SAC in 1931 in recognition of their financial stake in the organization, and neither SAC nor the *Varsity* could have remained solvent without the consent of their female constituents to such taxation. At University College, women students were similarly able to use their money to gain access to the Junior Common Room and, further, to acquire a stake in the Lit. itself.

The separate sphere collapsed very swiftly and with little debate in 1958,[24] leaving the question open as to whether it had been artificially propped up by those who had a personal interest in the concept, such as the dean of women, Marion Ferguson. The *in loco parentis* ideal of the university lasted far longer for women than it did for men. As Paul Axelrod puts it, "university authorities, playing the role of sub-stitute parents, felt obliged to uphold the virtue and morality of the women in their charge,"[25] and women in a separate sphere could be more easily watched and regulated.[26] In extracurricular life, however, increasingly fewer women students desired such separation, especially after 1945. The women who would force their way into Hart House in the late 1960s were simply acting upon a philosophy that had been articulated a generation earlier.

In general society, female university graduates continued to face serious obstacles. Although they had gained entry to traditionally male professions decades earlier, their attempts to use those rights were still resented and their positions in the professions were still marginalized. As high school teachers they possessed the strength of numbers, but this was often seen as a threat by male educators. Professional women were considered to be incompetent wives, and those who attempted to combine both roles had to deal with societal prejudices. Prentice and her associates note that "By the end of the 1950s, it should have been clear that women were in the workplace to stay. Instead, what was mainly noticed was the continuing emphasis on women's role in the home."[27] At the same time, their university education was not considered to be an asset if they were to become wives and mothers. In a sense there was no way to win in this situation: either women graduates became good wives and mothers and thus faced the criticism of those who saw their degrees as a waste of valuable state resources, or they became professionals and were criticized for treading on male domains, especially in times of economic crisis.[28]

Through their university experiences these women had already steeled themselves to some extent against criticism. After spending years fighting for a place in University College, these graduates were well prepared to struggle for a place in greater society. Many of them, though, did not join the fight, choosing instead to settle down to a traditional life of marriage and motherhood. Likewise, it should be noted, many men who governed the Lit. did not carry out the ideals that it professed. Nevertheless, the experience of serving as an officer on the WUA gave women more options, just as a university education was intended to when it was proposed for women in the 1880s. If certain options were not aggressively pursued, this cannot be used as a criticism of the organizations that attempted to provide them, especially considering the magnitude of the problem educated women faced in reconciling their university experiences with the actual society that confronted them.[29]

The officers of the Women's Undergraduate Association from 1922 to 1959, then, constituted a group of largely Toronto-born and educated white, Anglo-Saxon, protestants. They had inherited the idea of a separate sphere from an earlier generation and attempted to perpetuate it, often without the support of the rest of the female students of University College. The dignity and domesticity that informed WUA activities were no doubt connected to the domestic roles these students were expected to assume after graduation. But a critical mass of University College women rejected this ideology and sought out instead the company of men and a greater equality in the running of student affairs. By 1959 this made the continuation of the WUA impossible.

The women who pressed successfully for change on the University of Toronto campus did not have the same success carrying ideas of equality into their future careers. They were still largely faced with a choice between marriage or a public career, and most opted for marriage, after which they largely dropped out of public consciousness. Those who eschewed marriage were limited in their future career choices: outside of the high schools they faced tremendous barriers to entering many professions. Some of the women who led the WUA through the tangled relations with the Literary and Athletic Society were able then to find a way through the marriage-vs.-career conundrum and manage to combine the two paths. Others were able to break down some of the institutional barriers that kept them out of certain professions. In general, however, as far as can be determined from the data available (which are in almost every case inadequate for women in this period), the barriers outside the university were harder to break down than the door to the Junior Common Room.

7 Lives In Progress:
Lit. Officers, 1959–73

ORIGINS

The sheer number of university graduates after World War II made it next to impossible for alumni record keepers to collect more than rudimentary data about them, and it therefore became easier for individual graduates to slip through the cracks. For this period I had to glean information by questionnaire and anecdote. Graduates' suspicion about the University of Toronto's extensive fundraising process, however, made questionnaires a less-than-productive approach. The number of entries tagged with a question mark in the database, combined with my desire to use the same rigour in confirming these data as I had for the earlier periods, leaves tremendous gaps.

Anecdotal information about the former officers of the Literary and Athletic Society from 1959 to 1973 did, nevertheless, provide some interesting stories. A recent debate over a vacant Ontario seat on the Supreme Court of Canada seemed at one point to be between supporters of Rosalie Abella and those of John Laskin.[1] Both of these candidates were officers of this Lit. cohort (and neither got the job). Pharmaceutical advertisement regulations were discussed in the *Toronto Star*, and the expert source was Dr Joel Lexchin, an ex-officer of the Lit.[2] Canadian political figures Bob Rae, Peter McCreath, Barbara McDougall, Susan Eng, Sarmite Bulte – all served as officers between 1959 and 1973. For an organization that prided itself on leadership training, these are impressive results.

The Lit. also provided at least one shining example of the "turn on, tune in, drop out" school of student life in the 1960s, one who recently took up many pages of a study of the baby boom generation in Canada. He was listed without fanfare on the walls of the JCR as "D. DePoe," a first-year representative in 1965. David DePoe did not find the Lit., or the university, to his liking, and abandoned his middle-class upbringing as a son of a CBC broadcaster to take to the streets in an effort to preserve the bohemian culture of Yorkville against the authority of Metro Toronto. He thus landed a starring role in the NFB documentary on the subject, *Flowers on a One-Way Street*.[3] DePoe was also occasionally interviewed by the University of Toronto student press, for example in 1967 when he told the *Varsity*, "Two years ago student power in the university just wasn't possible, but today it is. This is because of hippie involvement."[4] DePoe believed this, and returned to University College in the 1970s to finish his degree. While there, he continued to agitate, and during a protest over the firing of a library worker he was assessed $140 for damage and threatened with a five-year prison term for "willful damage," charges he claimed were political and stemmed from his support of the Maoist Canadian Party of Labour.[5] Despite these difficulties DePoe survived the issue and finished his studies.

DePoe was one of the 277 students who served as officers on the University College Lit. from 1959 to 1973. One hundred and eighty-two were men, and ninety-five were women. The fears expressed by amalgamation opponents in the 1950s ended up coming true: the women of the college were outnumbered two to one on the Lit. executive.

Table 7.1 contrasts the varied geographic origins of the men as opposed to the more homogeneous birthplaces of the women. For the first time since the nineteenth century, a significant number of students were born outside of North America, 18% of the men falling into that category. The women, meanwhile, continued to come from Canada, and overwhelmingly from Toronto. A new wave of European immigration in the wake of population displacements caused by World War II, combined with the traditional immigrant impulse to educate males first, no doubt accounted for this difference.[6]

In terms of parental occupation (table 7.2), the profiles for men and women are also slightly different. Although nearly equal in the professional and business categories, the genders diverged at other economic ranks. More men had parents who were in supervisory and artisanal occupations, while the women had more parents, proportionally, in white-collar occupations. New, as well, was the larger number of semi- and unskilled fathers sending their children to university, representing the broadening availability of university education to society in general. Of course, this expansion was far less than the complete equality of educational opportunity sought by some reformers, which Paul Axelrod describes as "almost an article of faith among liberally minded citizens and politicians in the 1960s."[7]

The religious data for this period was successfully obscured by progressive tendencies in student record-keeping. Although registration forms at University College still asked for religious affiliation, the data was not transferred to students' records. Adding to the problem, a complete collection of registration forms does not exist, leaving gaps in the data. Because of affiliations reported in *Torontonensis* and certain other biographical sources, it is possible to state that the percentage of Jewish students on the Lit. rose dramatically, to 25% of the men and 22% of the women. Any objections to Jewish representation in student governance that might have existed in the 1930s and 1940s completely disappeared by the 1960s.

CAMPUS LIFE

In terms of their studies (table 7.3), the divergences between men and women persisted. Men continued to be more prominent in political science, mathematics, and commerce, while women showed similar proportional strength in the English and sociology/psychology streams. The figures for women in the general course were also significantly higher than for men. The situation was eventually muddied, though, by the creation of the "new programme" in the early 1970s that did away with the honours/general divide and instead moved to a simple three-year or four-year degree. Course analysis from 1970 on is a treacherous pursuit.

The student press occasionally commented upon the issue of education for women. At a Hart House debate in 1965 Professor J.S. Dupre of the Department of Political Economy "pointed out that women in the university are primarily there as a consumptive commodity, to while away their time before marriage." The *Gargoyle*, while not exactly supporting this position, commented:

Three or four years at university often leaves a woman in the paradoxical position of having been given an expensive education which indirectly results in her not having to work upon marriage. One question that the advocates of free tuition and others must answer is, then, whether the university investment is justified in the case of the female of our society ... is the society which neglects the potential of about half of its members as it clings to outmoded tradition itself at fault?[8]

The *Varsity* drove this point home when it reported, the next day, that the first woman president of SAC, Mary Brewin, was engaged to be married, "the fifth consecutive SAC president who has either become engaged or married during his (or her) term in office."[9] And in 1968, the *Varsity* observed:

in the JCR, the mini-skirts are so short that if a girl's slip starts to show you can no longer see her appendix scar. In the JCR, if the lipstick is smeared, it's probably a girl ... The JCR is where you go when you're a teaching fellow, and you've just learned to smoke Balkan Sobranie, because you want to meet that little Leslie in the back row of your tutorial who, you have heard, is a son of a gun. The best thing about the JCR is the shape of the girls ... A JCR girl beggars couth description, unless you have swung a half-empty sack of Irish cobblers.[10]

To what extent this sort of hyperbole described a real situation is unclear. Doug Owram cautions against using sources from the United States to judge Canadian sexual proclivities, but then declares "Various studies throughout the decade demonstrated that the most powerful force affecting sexual behaviour was the attitude of the peer group ... And this was a generation that, from the time of Davy Crocket, Barbie, and Dick Clark, had seen their peer group as North America."[11] That being said, Owram can provide no hard Canadian sources for any change in traditional attitudes toward sex on the Canadian campus, while I can only quote *Varsity* articles that continued to objectify women. If any real equality was afforded to women in this period, it was provided by the successful fight by women to gain access to Hart House, which yielded membership rights to women in 1972. As if to acknowledge the victory, in 1972/73 University College elected its first female president, and the year after ceased referring to them as "Miss" on the walls of the JCR.

CAREER PATHS

Over half the career data on the officers of the Lit. during this period are missing. This proportion rises to two-thirds for the women. Those officers for whom post-university occupations can be determined are overwhelmingly the professionals, who are easier to track. Fewer than a dozen (depending on the period after graduation) are known to have pursued non-professional business careers. This seems to be an under-representation, but it is impossible to be sure.

Of the 277 former officers, 52 (including 8 women) are known to have embarked on legal careers. Some of these ascended to high positions in the judiciary, five currently serving as judges on the Ontario Court of Appeals, and one on the British Columbia Supreme Court. One other, Barbara Betcherman, quit her legal career to become a novelist, although she published only one book, *Suspicions*, before being run over and killed while crossing a street in California. Two other lawyers also had significant media careers, Edward Greenspan and Hart Pomeranz (the original host of Global Television's *Grumps*).

There was a degree of cultural carry-over between the activities of the Lit. and the careers of its former officers. Beyond the three lawyers in the media, there were also three journalists, one director of marketing at a newspaper, three writers, an art gallery curator, several television executives, at least one playwright, and a museum consultant. These cultural occupation numbers, however, must be considered alongside five accountants, one actuary, thirty-four academics (twenty-five in universities), ten physicians, and two scientists. A few new occupations were also gaining university-trained leaders: among the known professionals were one systems analyst and two labour relations experts. In addition, there was one clergyman.

The figures for employment of the female officers of the Lit. (many of whom are included in the totals above) are generally not well documented. Of the ninety-five, only thirty-one are known to have been employed ten years after graduation. Among the large group of missing cases are twenty-eight who married (for the whole group, 59 women [62%] are known to have married), but in only four cases are the marriage dates extant. The thirty-one who were employed highlight some possible trends. Seven (22.6%) found work in the legal profession, one as a family court judge. This percentage was higher than for any other period. Thirteen were in education; five of these taught at universities, all apparently at the assistant professor level or lower. Rounding out the group were a librarian, two consultants, a researcher, a social worker, a systems analyst, two writers, an art gallery employee, and an investment analyst. Especially noteworthy is the fact that twenty-five of the thirty-one are known to have been married while pursuing their careers, showing that by the 1960s the stigma against combining the two had been nearly eliminated.

Yet another sex-gender stigma lessened during this period. At least one former officer of the Lit. from this period has formally "come out," declaring himself a homosexual. Another, whose sexual orientation is not known, criticized the questionnaire design used in researching this book as being "heterosexual" in its orientation. These issues are completely absent from any information collected for the pre-1960s cohorts.[12]

The absence of data makes other comments about Lit. officers difficult. However, some studies of university students and careers in this period describe the possibilities available for employment for this group. The most ambitious of these, *Education and Employment of Arts and Science Graduates: The Last Decade in Ontario*, was prepared for the Commission on Post-Secondary Education in Ontario in 1972 by Edward Harvey of the Ontario Institute for Studies in Education. Harvey sent questionnaires to over 4,000 bachelors-level graduates from 1960 to 1968 at the University of Toronto, Queen's University, McMaster University, and the University of Waterloo, and received a response rate of 64%. Among his findings was that only 29% of the respondents considered their undergraduate education to be "relevant" to the labour market they had entered.[13] However, graduates did find themselves in reasonably prestigious positions. Harvey's categories for employment are quite different than the ones used for this study, and he noted that nearly 50% of the graduates had located their first jobs in the academic system, with most of those becoming elementary or secondary school teachers. Another 10% entered various ranks of the civil service.[14]

One of Harvey's main conclusions was that as the 1960s progressed, graduates found it harder to find prestigious jobs, and that their prospects for career advancement were negligible.[15] The situation did not improve for graduates of the early 1970s. The 1971 study, *The Market Situation for University Graduates: Canada*, declared "the national market situation is characterized by an overall state of excess supply for both B.A. and M.A. graduates – approximately 47 percent of B.A. graduates and 70 percent of M.A. graduates." The study did note that the problem of oversupply was least acute in Ontario,[16] but certainly university graduates were finding that the mass-produced degrees of the 1960s and 1970s were of less value in their later careers than had previous cohorts.

Paul Axelrod observes that there was a growing trend, beginning around 1968, to question the return on investment in the university sector and to claim that educated individuals performed many jobs less effectively than others did.[17] Rising unemployment made the expansion plans of the universities seem out of place with the requirements of society in general. Too many graduates were now being produced for an economy that did not need them.[18]

DISILLUSION AND CHANGE

In the 1960s and early 1970s Canadian universities were under attack from both within and without. Although they had entered the 1960s as institutions with a great deal of societal support, dedicated to the provision of a trained elite in a society that seemed to require more educated individuals, they began the 1970s as institutions taking in a great deal of public money and producing graduates that, it seemed, few people wanted. Simultaneously on the inside, every tradition the university system held dear was under attack by a large group of students who were accustomed to getting their own way in society. Students were continually told that the university was the epitome of human values, a place where ideas were challenged and society improved through discussion and inquiry. Instead, many entered large, anonymous institutions where what and how they were taught seemed to have little relevance to the problems of modernity.

The Lit. struggled against the various forces of individual interest, political activism, and mass alienation that were arrayed together at the University of Toronto during this period, but on the whole found these forces too strong. Although attempting several times to stay relevant and remain attuned to the concerns of the University College student body, the society eventually succumbed and became marginal to students' interests and affairs.

The lack of data on the future careers of those determined officers who kept the Lit. alive from 1959 to 1973 makes any general comments on the organization as a source for additional training difficult. It would be gratifying to be able to claim that the battles the Lit. officers of the 1960s and early 1970s fought prepared them to face the uncertainties of the job market into which they emerged, and this contention does have some anecdotal support. Further quantitative material will have to be located, however, before these anecdotes can be put in their proper context.

Conclusion

The last student covered in this book graduated from University College in 1977. The world he entered was quite different from that of the young men who founded the Literary and Scientific Society in 1854. The changes in Canadian society had been multitudinous, affecting the University of Toronto, its students, and their prospects. Students had moved from a world in which the occupational choices of university arts graduates were largely confined to the talking professions of the law, the clergy, and academia, to a society to which hundreds of possible options, including the media, accountancy, and consulting, had been added. Women, curiosities at universities when they first enrolled in 1884, had become a fixture in an unchallengeably coeducational environment. Although certain occupational choices were still more likely for women than they were for men, and the pressures of marriage and child-rearing were still apparent, much of the earlier stigma that co-eds suffered as late as 1945 had disappeared. Women could now combine marriage with a career, and especially a teaching career, without serious challenge or obvious hindrance. Equality had not been achieved, but much discrimination had been overcome.

By the beginning of the 1970s, however, both men and women, had new factors to contend with that were much different than those of earlier periods. While the number of university graduates had increased, the value of university degrees had decreased. The easy transition from professional training to professional success enjoyed by many lawyers and clergymen before 1921 was less obvious for the final cohort. Universities had been brought under public scrutiny in the 1960s and the issues of relevance and connection to capitalism raised in those years caused both students and the wider society to become less convinced of the utility of a university education.

University College as well had been transformed during the one hundred years under study. From a small institution that assimilated students from across Canada and beyond, the college had become a larger entity but, at the same time, a more parochial one, educating people from a shrinking catchment area. Although the geographic range of these students narrowed, their social spectrum increased, as more people from lower ranks of society and different religious groups found a place in the academic cloisters. Despite these changes, however, throughout every period students from professional and business backgrounds were the dominant members of the undergraduate body.

Since its founding the University of Toronto has functioned as an institution for the promotion of social mobility. Before 1921, the sons and, to a lesser extent, the daughters, of farmers were present in large numbers. They entered as farmers and left as professionals. In later periods, significant numbers of students from artisanal and white-collar backgrounds have been present at the university and have used the experience as a means to improve their socio-economic status. The university aided the transition of Ontario (and Canada) from a rural to an urban society.

University College also preserved and produced a professional class, and to that extent also a middle class. The degree to which the graduates of University College can unequivocally be declared middle class is less clear than could be desired. Further research and analysis of a larger student population would improve this situation. Among other things, this book has demonstrated that the possibilities of quantitative analysis of university students have by no means been exhausted.

Issues of access, gender relations, social mobility, and career advancement continue to be part of the ongoing debate about the place of higher education in Canadian society. While the debate rages, students continue to share the same essential features: they come from somewhere, and they go to somewhere. I hope that this book has shown that the comings and goings are as important, if not more so, than the time spent in between.

APPENDICES

APPENDIX A

The History of the JCR Wall

The Lit. displays the names of its officers for all to see on the walls of the Junior Common Room (JCR) of University College at the University of Toronto. The names of all the officers of the Literary and Scientific Society, Literary and Athletic Society, Women's Literary Society, and Women's Undergraduate Association, from 1854 to the present, are emblazoned in gold leaf across all four walls of the room.

This does not mean that in 1854 the Lit. recognized that it would be looked upon as an organization worthy of gilded treatment. The names were first placed on the walls of the JCR in 1926, shortly after the Literary and Athletic Society gained possession of the space. Before that date, the room had served in different eras as a residence dining hall, classroom, and administrative office for the university. After the construction of Simcoe Hall in 1923, the location was no longer needed for the central administration of the university, and it was rechristened the Junior Common Room.

Around that time a young student named Egerton Brown located "old records" that included the "names of Canadians who later had become leaders in various careers in Canada." Brown suggested the names be inscribed on panels on the walls of the JCR, and the Lit agreed.[1] Brown's lists were less than perfect – the first group of names on the wall contains several spelling errors and some officers were assigned to the wrong years – but after that point the Lit. yearly inscribed the names of the men who served.

After 1959, when the Lit. and the WUA merged into one organization, the names of both male and female officers were added to the list. This marked the first appearance of female names on the JCR wall, the women until 1973 being identified as "Miss" so as to set them apart from the men.[2] In 1989, after a major renovation of the room, the names of the officers of the WLS and WUA before 1959 were located and also added. Since 1990, the JCR wall has therefore been a full compendium of elected student leaders at University College from the foundation of the institution.

The JCR walls are a rare historical document.[3] Not only do they provide a list of over a century of university students, but they also speak to a college ideology that considered this information so worthy of preservation that gold leaf was expended in the effort.

APPENDIX B
Study Methodology

The names of all 1,876 members of the various organizations were entered into a database. Biographical information on these students was then collected. This methodology was derived from J.K. Johnson's study of leadership in Upper Canada.[1] Johnson used the biographies of the men elected to the Upper Canadian House of Assembly as a means to sketch a collective biography of Upper Canadians, specifically concentrating on the preconditions necessary for election to office. Johnson collected data on "birth and death, family relationships, education, religious denomination, occupation, residence, land holding, military service, appointed office-holding and (of course) provincial political office."[2]

Although Johnson was working backward from public prominence, while the present study ranges forward from participation on the Lit., the general biographical details sought were remarkably similar. Some issues (e.g., land-holding) were dropped and other data on occupational type and location that seemed necessary to evaluate the contributions of former Lit. members were added. Twenty-five separate pieces of information were needed to assemble each case, and although very few are complete, on balance enough information was found to evaluate quantitatively the biography of the societies, just as Johnson found enough information to evaluate the road to political power in Upper Canada.

The information was collected from diverse sources, which resulted in many methodological problems. In the records consulted, several students were given two different birthplaces, two sets of parents, and sometimes different death dates and places. Some degree of common sense was used when the sources were not clear. On occasion students were not positively identified in the sources, and in the case of Wilbur Grant the failure of any obituary to link him with the university means that his file is completely blank. In another instance, it was nearly impossible to distinguish between two Alexander Sutherlands who attended the university at the same time, but eventually one was chosen by inference from the sources available.

Further difficulties ensued about how to code and define occupational information. A significant discussion of this is found in Paul Axelrod's *Making a Middle Class*, and his system of classification was followed in the hopes of establishing some standard against which future studies can be made.[3]

Most significant, however, are several source biases in the data collected. Information located in Toronto was in general easier to find than in the rest of Ontario, records in Ontario easier than in Canada, and data in Canada easier than in the rest of the world. Information on men was easier to discover than on women, which speaks to the imperfect coeducation of the university and its alumni association. Records of professional men were easier to find than for businessmen, and information on successful people was easier to locate than on unsuccessful ones. The tracking system of the University of Toronto Alumni Association, by virtue its dependence on newspaper report and personal volunteering of information, was of necessity selective, and no amount of extra work can completely redress this situation.

The pre-1959 students were coded by sex and graduation cohort. For the men, three temporal division points were established. 1890 was chosen as the first division point largely because of a fire that did significant damage to the college in February of that year. It also marked a transition in the history of the University of Toronto, because a new University Act of 1887 allowed for other colleges to federate with the university, thereby diluting University College's role as the sole teaching institution for arts students. The next division point, 1921, was also chosen because of college events. It marked the demise of the Literary and Scientific Society and the creation of the Literary and Athletic Society. For Canada as a whole, 1921 is seen as a moment of transition from an agrarian to an urban society. The third division point, 1959, although completely arbitrary in terms of Canadian society, marked the end of separate male and female student societies at University College.

These temporal markers established three distinct groups of men prior to 1959 and one mixed group after. For ease of comparison, periodization for the women was kept the same. The database is thus divided into seven cohorts: men, 1854–90; men, 1891–1921; women, 1891–1921; men, 1922–58; women, 1922–58; men, 1959–73; and women, 1959–73.

Tables

Table 2.1
Place of birth, Lit. officers, 1854–90

	No.	Percentage
Toronto and environs	72	28
Southwestern Ontario	63	25
Eastern Ontario	36	14
Other Ontario	23	9
Quebec	6	2
Maritimes	5	2
Other Canada	7	3
United States	5	2
British Isles	35	14
Other	3	1
Unknown	63	

Note: Some tables do not add up to 100% because of rounding.

Table 2.2
Father's occupation category, Lit. officers, 1854–90

	No.	Percentage
Professional	85	35
Business	40	16
Supervisory	8	3
White collar	14	6
Artisan-Skilled	24	10
Semi-/Unskilled	2	1
Farming-Fishing	69	29
Unknown	77	

Table 2.3
Religious affiliation, Lit. officers, 1854–90

	No.	Percentage
Anglican	92	34
Presbyterian	112	41
Methodist	38	14
Baptist	13	5
Roman Catholic	4	1
Other Christian	12	5
Unknown	48	

Table 2.4
Occupation category after 10/30 years, Lit. officers, 1854–90

	10 years		30 years	
	No.	Percentage	No.	Percentage
Professional	237	83	193	65
Business	11	4	13	4
Supervisory	3	1	8	3
White collar	2	1	5	2
Semi-/Unskilled	1	0.5	0	0
Student	1	0.5	1	0.5
Dead	29	10	74	25
Unknown	34		24	

Table 2.5
Location after 10/30 years, Lit. officers, 1854–90

	10 years		30 years	
	No.	Percentage	No.	Percentage
Toronto and environs	109	45	108	50
Southwestern Ontario	36	15	23	11
Eastern Ontario	22	9	16	7
Other Ontario	17	7	12	6
Quebec	6	2	3	1
Manitoba	13	5	11	5
British Columbia	7	3	8	4
Other Canada	4	2	6	3
United States	24	10	22	10
British Isles	4	2	4	2
India and Japan	3	1	2	1
Unknown	74		104	

Table 2.6
University graduates holding headmasterships at Ontario high schools,
1866–85

Year	Heads	Toronto	Victoria	Trinity	Queen's	Misc.
1866	104	16	3	4	5	76
1870	101	33	13	8	8	39
1876	104	45	21	3	9	26
1880	105	50	22	3	11	19
1885	103	58	20	9	12	4

Source: Varsity, 14 February 1885. Victoria includes Albert College. Misc. includes
all non-university educated teachers.

Table 3.1
Place of birth, Lit. officers, 1891–1921

	No.	Percentage
Toronto and environs	92	26
Southwestern Ontario	109	31
Eastern Ontario	42	12
Rest of Ontario	80	23
Manitoba	6	2
Other Canada	2	1
United States	8	2
British Isles	8	2
Rest of world	3	1
Unknown	29	

Table 3.2
Father's occupation category, Lit. officers, 1891–1921

	No.	Percentage
Professional	95	28
Business	83	25
Supervisory	14	4
White collar	26	8
Artisan-Skilled	27	8
Semi-/Unskilled	3	1
Farming-Fishing	85	25
Student	1	neg.
Unknown	45	

Note: "neg." signifies negligible.

Table 3.3
Religious affiliation, Lit. officers, 1891–1921

	No.	Percentage
Anglican	80	22
Presbyterian	170	47
Methodist	57	16
Baptist	13	4
Roman Catholic	20	6
Other Christian	18	5
Jewish	3	1
Unknown	18	

Table 3.4
Occupation category after 10/30 years, Lit. officers, 1891–1921

	10 years		30 years	
	No.	Percentage	No.	Percentage
Professional	257	75	213	63
Business	17	5	32	9
Supervisory	26	8	26	8
White collar	8	2	5	2
Artisan-Skilled	6	2	3	1
Farming/Fishing	3	1	2	1
Student	1	neg.	2	1
Deceased	24	7	55	16
Unknown	37		41	

Table 3.5
Location after 10/30 years, Lit. officers, 1891–1921

	10 years		30 years	
	No.	Percentage	No.	Percentage
Toronto and environs	95	30	102	36
Southwestern Ontario	47	15	29	10
Eastern Ontario	19	6	28	10
Other Ontario	18	6	12	4
Quebec	12	4	12	4
Manitoba	14	4	10	4
Saskatchewan	7	2	5	2
Alberta	19	6	19	6
British Columbia	10	3	14	5
Maritimes	5	2	1	neg.
Other Canada	3	1	2	1
United States	45	14	37	13
British Isles	11	3	5	2
Rest of world	11	3	5	2
Unknown	63		98	

Table 3.6
Professional occupation after 10 years, Lit. officers,
1891–1921

	No.	Percentage
Lawyer	81	26
Clergyman	44	14
Physician	28	9
Teacher/Professor	59	19
Journalist	11	4
Engineer	14	5
Scientist	10	3
Accountant	6	2
Other	2	0.6

Note: Percentages are calculated on 309 cases, excluding
46 unknown and 24 deceased.

Table 3.7
Intended occupation, Lit. officers, 1904–21, and number who matched
their intentions 10 years after graduation

	No. Intended	No. Matched	Percentage Matched
Lawyer	37	23	62
Clergyman	14	10	71
Physician	8	8	100
Teacher/Professor	10	5	50
Journalist	1	0	0
Actuary	3	0	0
Businessman	2	0	0
Surveyor	1	0	0

Note: Eight of the students were dead by this point.

Table 3.8
Occupation of all Lit. officers, 1891–1921, who resided in Toronto
and environs 20 years after graduation

	· No.		No.
Law	26	Secretary treasurer	3
Clergyman	10	Manager	7
Teacher/Professor	17	Superintendent	2
Physician	11	Staff, Abattoir	1
Journalist	8	Asst. Hotel manager	1
Scientist	2	Business secretary	1
Actuary	2	Civil servant	1
Engineer	6	Publisher's rep.	1
Businessman	11	Unknown	2

TOTAL: 112

Table 3.9
University presidents/College principals, Lit. officers, 1891–1921

	Occupation	Institution
George H. Black	President	Rutgers University
David S. Dix	Acting Principal	St. Andrew's College, Saskatoon
Frederick B.R. Hellems	Acting President	Colorado State University
George G.D. Kilpatrick	Principal	United Theological College, Montreal
Milton E. Liezert	Principal	Alberta College of Education
Robert D. McElheran	Principal	Wycliffe College, Toronto
John McKay	Principal	United Theological College, Manitoba
James A. McLean	Founding President	University of Manitoba
John McNicol	Principal	Toronto Bible College
James A. Sharrard	Principal	Indore College, Indore, India
David Thomson	Acting President	University of Washington, Seattle
William H. Vance	Principal	Westminster Theological College, Vancouver

Table 3.10
Actuarial and life insurance careers, Lit. officers, 1891–1921

	Company	Dates
Charles H. Armstrong	Imperial Life Assurance	1904–1953
Ernest R. Brock	Great West Life	1920–1957
David E. Kilgour	North American Life	1905–1946 (President 1939)
John M. Laird	Connecticut General Life	1907–1942 (Vice-president 1927)
Isaac P. McNabb	Dominion Life Insurance	1921–1961
Edward E. Reid	London Life Insurance	1895–1941 (Vice-president 1932)
John S. Thompson	Mutual Life Insurance	1910–1926
	Mutual Benefit of Newark	1926–1953 (President 1946)
William A.P. Wood	Canada Life Assurance	1899–1938

Table 4.1
Place of birth, WLS/WUA officers, 1891–1921

	No.	Percentage
Toronto and environs	70	37
Southwestern Ontario	46	24
Eastern Ontario	14	7
Other Ontario	37	20
Maritimes	4	2
Other Canada	4	2
United States	7	4
British Isles	5	3
Rest of world	2	1
Unknown	22	

Table 4.2
Father's occupation category, WLS/WUA officers,
1891–1921

	No.	Percentage
Professional	63	31
Business	63	31
Supervisory	19	10
White collar	18	9
Artisan-Skilled	20	10
Semi-/Unskilled	1	0.5
Farming-Fishing	16	8
Unknown	11	

Table 4.3
Religious affiliation, WLS/WUA officers, 1891–1921

	No.	Percentage
Anglican	36	18
Presbyterian	113	55
Methodist	30	15
Baptist	10	5
Roman Catholic	9	4
Other Christian	6	3
Jewish	2	1
Unknown	5	

Table 4.4
Course of study, WLS/WUA officers, 1891–1921, compared to Lit. officers

	WLS/WUA		Lit.	
	No.	Percentage	No.	Percentage
Political Science	5	2.4	104	27.4
History	8	3.8	8	2.1
Philosophy	2	0.9	41	10.8
English	32	15.2	14	3.7
Moderns	70	33.2	12	3.2
Classics	14	6.6	30	7.9
Math/Physics	13	6.2	43	11.3
Natural Science	4	1.9	29	7.7
Chemistry & Mineralogy	0	0	13	3.4
Household Science	9	4.3	0	0
General/Pass	44	20.9	43	11.3
Law	0	0	1	0.3
Commerce	0	0	1	0.3
Engineering	0	0	18	4.7
Unknown	10	4.7	22	5.8

Table 4.5
Registrations in Faculty of Arts courses, 1912/13

	No. Men	No. Women	Preponderant Gender	
Political Science	72	0	Men	100
History	10	1	Men	95
Philosophy	41	3	Men	90
English	30	55	Women	64
Moderns	11	78	Women	87
Classics	20	9	Men	66
Math/Physics	57	21	Men	73
Natural Science	60	4	Men	94
Commerce	27	0	Men	100
Chemistry	24	0	Men	100
Geology	5	0	Men	100
Forestry	5	0	Men	100
Household Science	0	33	Women	100
General	287	124	Men	70

Note: There were 1,078 students at University College in 1912/13, of whom 709,
or 65%, were men.
Source: Adapted from *President's Report* (1912/13), 38–9. Certain courses have
been added together to simplify comparisons. "Greek and Hebrew" and
"Orientals," for example, have been combined with "Classics." Natural Science
includes "Physiol. and Bioch. Sci.," "Biology," and "Natural and Physical
Sciences." Natural and Physical Sciences had only male students.

Table 4.6
Husband's occupation, WLS/WUA officers, 1891–1921

	No.		No.
Businessman	27	Engineer	4
Clergyman	12	Politician	1
Teacher/Professor	12	Organist	1
Physician	12	Superintendent	1
Lawyer	10	Writer	1
Actuary	5	Soldier	1
Journalist	5	Farmer	1
Civil servant	4		

Table 4.7
WLS/WUA officers, 1891–1921, by number of children

No. children	No. officers	Percentage of officers
0	127	60
1	28	13
2	28	13
3	14	7
4	11	5
5+	3	2

Table 4.8
Children of Lit. officers, 1891–1921, who married
(Figures for WLS/WUA 1891–1921, in parentheses)

	Percentage
No children	42.5 (32)
One child	12.9 (23)
Two children	16.1 (23)
Three childdren	15.0 (11)
Four children	7.1 (9)
Five or more children	6.4 (2)

Note: The marital status of 20.9% of all Lit. officers,
1891–1921, is not known.

Table 4.9
Occupation category after 10/30 years, WLS/WUA officers, 1891–1921

	10 years		30 years	
	No.	Percentage	No.	Percentage
Professional	70	50	45	38
Business	0	0	1	1
Supervisory	1	1	6	5
White collar	14	10	5	4
Mother/Housewife	47	33	39	33
Student	2	1	1	1
Deceased	7	5	21	18
Unknown	70		93	

Table 4.10
Location after 10/30 years, WLS/WUA officers, 1891–1921

	10 years		30 years	
	No.	Percentage	No.	Percentage
Toronto and environs	56	41	57	52
Southwestern Ontario	14	10	14	13
Other Ontario	15	11	4	4
Other Canada	18	14	13	12
United States	22	16	16	15
Rest of world	10	7	6	5
Unknown	76		101	

Table 4.11
Careers, Canadian women graduates, 1884–1917

Institution	Women Graduates	Married	Teaching	Other Profession	Business	Unaccounted
University College	1,271	370	296	165	62	378
Victoria	420	142	115	75	19	69
Trinity	208	67	41	31	12	66
McMaster	189	66	72	12	7	32
McGill	488	179	173	75	14	47
Queen's	697	192	175	40	11	279
Western	44	9	26	5	1	3
University of Manitoba	287	93	21	13	2	158
University of Saskatchewan	47	10	24	9	1	3
University of Alberta	44	10	20	7	3	4
University of British Columbia	56	1	39	6	3	7
TOTALS	3,751	1,139	1,002	438	135	1,046

Source: McPherson, "Careers of Canadian University Women," 19A. McPherson attempted to get responses from a Maritime university but none responded.

Table 4.12
University College women in "professions other than teaching,"
1884–1917

	No.		No.
Medicine	30	Civil service	14
Law	10	Dietetics	11
Nursing	12	Secretarial	6
Journalism	5	Missionary	6
University Work	21	Further Study	3
Library	23	Other	7
Social work	17		

Source: McPherson, "Careers of Canadian University Women," 28A.

Table 4.13
Occupation, WLS/WUA officers, 1891–1921

	After 5 years	After 10 years
	No.	No.
High School Teacher	50	39
Other Teacher	13	5
University Lecturer	3	2
University Professor	1	2
Dean of Residence	0	1
Scientific Researcher	2	2
Journalist	4	3
Missionary	3	3
Social Worker	2	0
Musician	1	0
Nurse	1	3
Dietician	0	1
Librarian	0	2
Lawyer	0	1
Law student	0	1
Factory manager	1	0
Factory inspector	0	1
Girl's work secretary	2	1
Clerk/Secretary	15	14

Table 5.1
Place of birth, Lit. officers, 1922–58

	No.	Percentage
Toronto and environs	165	52
Southwestern Ontario	42	13
Eastern Ontario	17	5
Rest of Ontario	32	10
Quebec	4	1
Manitoba	8	3
Saskatchewan	8	3
Alberta	8	3
British Columbia	4	1
Other Canada	2	1
United States	13	4
Rest of world	11	3
Unknown	4	

Table 5.2
Father's occupation category, Lit. officers, 1922–58

	No.	Percentage
Professional	98	32
Business	105	34
Supervisory	30	10
White collar	29	10
Artisan-Skilled	26	9
Semi-/Unskilled	4	1
Farming-Fishing	12	4
Unknown	14	

Table 5.3
Parents' occupation category, 971 Faculty of Arts
students, 1927

	No.	Percentage
Professional	232	23.9
Business	287	29.6
Managerial	30	3.1
Clerical	110	11.3
Skilled labour	86	8.9
Unskilled	not a category	
Farming	92	9.5
Miscellaneous	23	2.4
Retired	25	2.6
Deceased	76	7.8
Unspecified	10	1.0

Source: Adapted by the author from an initial study by Kemp,
President's Report (1927/28), 11–12. Kemp did not count
unskilled workers, and it is unknown exactly what the
"Miscellaneous" category contained. Kemp apparently never
completed his final study.

Table 5.4
Parents' occupation category, 3,682 university students,
1935/36

	Percentage
Professional	27.1
Business	27.3
Supervisory	11.7
White collar	10.0
Artisan-Skilled	7.9
Semi-skilled	5.2
Farming/Fishing	10.8

Source: Axelrod, *Making a Middle Class*, 23, table 4. Figures
include 707 Dalhousie students, 1,320 University of Toronto
students, 1,437 University of Alberta students, and 218
Queen's students. The occupational categories in this book
follow Axelrod's analysis.

Table 5.5
Religious affiliation, Lit. officers, 1922–58

	No.	Percentage
Anglican	71	24
Presbyterian	49	17
Methodist	4	1
Baptist	13	4
United Church	71	24
Roman Catholic	9	3
Other Christian	28	9
Jewish	50	17
Unknown	23	

Table 5.6
Course of study, Lit. officers, 1922–58

	No.	Percentage
Political Science	66	21
Law	19	6
History	18	6
Philosophy	9	3
Sociology/Psychology	10	3
English	12	4
Moderns	2	1
Classics	6	2
Math/Physics/Chemistry	15	5
Natural Science	1	neg.
Commerce	59	19
Engineering	1	neg.
General/Pass	92	29
Physical/Health Education	4	1
No Degree	1	neg.
Unknown	3	

Table 5.7
Course of study, all University College students, 1925/26 and 1954/55

	1925/26		1954/55	
	No.	Percentage	No.	Percentage
Political Science	88	7	56	4.7
Law	Only offered 1933–50			
History	21	2	65	5.4
Philosphy	32	2.5	59	5
Sociology/Psychology	1	0.1	60	5
English	82	6.5	56	4.7
Moderns	113	8.9	44	3.7
Classics	31	2.4	25	2.1
Math/Physics	99	7.8	96	8.1
Natural Science	94	7.4	52	4.3
Commerce	156	12.2	85	7.1
Pass/General	522	41	559	47

Source: Numbers for 1925/26 compiled from *President's Report* (1925/26), 97.
Numbers for 1954/55 compiled from *President's Report* (1954/5), 260. Certain
courses are combined in this table: for 1954/55, especially, the first year program
numbers for "Soc&Phil." students were divided among Political Science, History,
Philosophy, and Sociology/Psychology, the four programs to which this first-year
course were pre-requisites. "Pass" students are from 1925/26, "General" students
are from 1954/55. Note that in 1925/26, 56% of University College students were
male; 61% were male in 1954/55.

Table 5.8
Course streams, Lit. officers, 1922–58
(expressed in relation to father's occupation category)

	Percentage in political science	Percentage in commerce/general
Professional	25	33
Business	13	53
Supervisory	31	62
White collar	21	62
Artisan-Skilled	28	48
Semi-/Unskilled	25	50
Farming-Fishing	18	27

Table 5.9
Occupation category after 10/30 years, Lit. officers, 1922–58

	10 years		30 years	
	No.	Percentage	No.	Percentage
Professional	150	56	138	57
Business	38	14	46	19
Supervisory	39	15	25	10
White Collar	20	7	6	2
Artisan-Skilled	2	1	0	0
Semi-/Unskilled	3	1	0	0
Student	5	2	0	0
Dead	11	4	28	11
Unknown	50		75	

Table 5.10
Location after 10/30 years, Lit. officers, 1922–58

	10 years		30 years	
	No.	Percentage	No.	Percentage
Toronto and environs	158	61	136	63
Southwestern Ontario	24	9	16	8
Eastern Ontario	21	8	20	9
Rest of Ontario	8	3	6	3
Quebec	8	3	7	3
British Columbia	6	2	7	3
Other Canada	9	4	6	3
United States	11	4	11	5
Rest of world	13	5	6	3
Unknown	60		103	

Table 6.1
Place of birth, WUA officers, 1922–58

	No.	Percentage
Toronto and Environs	164	50
Southwestern Ontario	56	17
Eastern Ontario	18	5
Rest of Ontario	31	9
Quebec	10	3
Manitoba	6	2
Saskatchewan	6	2
Alberta	6	2
British Columbia	7	2
Other Canada	4	1
United States	12	4
Rest of world	9	3
Unknown	12	

Table 6.2
Father's occupation category, WUA officers, 1922–58

	No.	Percentage
Professional	148	45
Business	87	26
Supervisory	42	13
White collar	24	7
Artisan-Skilled	12	4
Semi-/Unskilled	2	1
Farming-Fishing	13	4
Unknown	13	

Table 6.3
Religious affiliation, WUA officers, 1922–58

	No.	Percentage
Anglican	101	31
Presbyterian	67	21
Methodist	8	2
Baptist	6	2
United Church	87	27
Roman Catholic	5	2
Other Christian	33	10
Jewish	13	4
Unknown	22	

Table 6.4
Course of study, WUA officers, 1922–58

	No.	Percentage
Political Science	7	2
History	16	5
Philosophy	15	5
Sociology/Psychology	26	8
English	38	11
Moderns	32	10
Classics	3	1
Math/Physics/Chemistry	3	1
Natural Science	7	2
Commerce	6	2
Household Science	33	10
General/Pass	135	40
Art	5	1
Physical/Health Education	11	3
Unknown	5	

Table 6.5
Occupation category after 10/30 years, WUA officers, 1922–58

	10 years		30 years	
	No.	Percentage	No.	Percentage
Professional	60	36	70	49
Business	0	0	4	3
Supervisory	4	2	4	3
White collar	21	13	14	10
Artisan-Skilled	1	1	2	1
Mother/Homemaker	73	44	37	26
Student	3	2	1	1
Deceased	3	2	12	8
Unknown	177		197	

Table 6.6
Location after 10/30 years, WUA officers, 1922–58

	10 years		30 years	
	No.	Percentage	No.	Percentage
Toronto and environs	107	56	93	57
Southwestern Ontario	23	12	19	12
Eastern Ontario	13	7	12	7
Rest of Ontario	9	5	11	7
Quebec	5	3	5	3
British Columbia	6	3	5	3
Other Canada	7	4	4	2
United States	16	8	12	7
Rest of world	6	3	3	2
Unknown	151			

Table 6.7
Higher degrees and marriage rates, WUA/WLS officers, 1891–1973

	1891–1921		1922–1958		1959–1973	
	No.	Percentage	No.	Percentage	No.	Percentage
Total officers	211		342		95	
Officers with higher degrees	33	16	58	17	13	14
Officers with higher degrees who married	14	42	47	81	12	92
DEGREES						
PhD	8		16		3	
MA	21		32		5	
MB	3		0		0	
BPaed	1		0		0	
MSc	0		4		0	
MEd	0		3		0	
MSW	0		2		2	
MLS	0		1		0	
MD	0		0		1	
MES	0		0		1	
MBA	0		0		1	

Table 6.8
WUA officers with children, 1922–58

No. of children	No. of officers	Percentage with children
0	145	42
1	32	9
2	57	17
3	59	17
4	29	8
5	14	4
6+	6	2

Table 7.1
Place of birth, men and women on Lit., 1959–73

	Men		Women	
	No.	Percentage	No.	Percentage
Toronto and environs	69	46	46	65
Southwestern Ontario	14	9	4	6
Eastern Ontario	6	4	4	6
Northern Ontario	6	4	1	1
Ontario – region unknown*	12	8	4	6
Other Canada	15	10	8	11
United States	2	1	1	1
Rest of world	26	18	3	4
Unknown	32		24	

*Beginning in the late 1960s, student records listed place of birth by province only. For women on the Lit., this figure includes one known to be born in Northern Ontario.

Table 7.2
Father's occupation category, men and women on Lit., 1959–73

	Men		Women	
	No.	Percentage	No.	Percentage
Professional	40	28	22	27
Business	48	34	33	41
Supervisory	18	13	7	9
White collar	12	9	10	12
Artisan-Skilled	18	13	5	6
Semi-/Unskilled	5	3	4	5
Farmer	1	1	0	0
Unknown	40		14	

Table 7.3
Course of study, men and women on Lit., 1959–73

	Men		Women	
	No.	Percentage	No.	Percentage
Political Science	27	16	3	3
History	22	13	9	11
Philosophy	11	7	2	2
Sociology/Psychology	12	7	17	20
English	9	5	11	13
Moderns	0	0	2	2
Classics	2	1	0	0
Math/Physics/Chemistry	17	10	1	1
Natural Science	6	4	0	0
Commerce	11	7	2	2
General/Pass	42	26	36	42
Physical/Health Education	1	1	0	0
Art	0	0	2	2
No Degree	5	3	2	2
Unknown	17		8	

Notes

INTRODUCTION

1 See for example, Fingard, "College, Career and Community," 26–50; Gaffield et al., "Student Populations and Graduate Careers," 3–25; Stewart, "*It's Up to You*; and the forthcoming study by Ruby Heap on women in engineering in Canada.
2 Axelrod, *Making a Middle Class.*
3 McKillop, *Matters of Mind.*

CHAPTER ONE

1 "The Literary and Athletic Society – A Fiftieth Anniversary," 136
2 Horn, *History of the University of Edinburgh*, 92–3, 142–3.
3 McLachlan, "The Choice of Hercules," 489. See also Harding, *College Literary Societies* and Simpson, "The Little Republics."
4 Bell, "The Lit. 1854–1934," 16
5 McLachlan, "The Choice of Hercules," 488–9.
6 *Constitution and Bylaws of the Literary and Scientific Society.*
7 Fred F. Manley to the Editor, *Varsity*, 13 March 1886.
8 Bell, "The Lit.," 19; see also *Saturday Night*, 23 February 1889: "Why could we not have dancing! ... Why is all this good music wasted year after year!"
9 See *Varsity*, 11 November 1881; 24 February 1882.
10 See *Varsity*, 18 February, 24 November 1883.

11 N.H. Russell to the Editor, *Varsity*, 13 February 1886.

12 H.C. Boultbee to the Editor, *Varsity*, 20 March 1887.

13 Or, as a group of non-partisan students stated in 1888, "We think that the Literary Society should be true to the purposes of its origin; and that in fulfilling any other function – such as instruction in political management and opposition – it goes beyond its proper sphere." See "Annual Elections of the Literary Society," March 1888, UTA/B65-0038/001(07).

14 College Council minutes, 21 October 1904, UTA/A69-0011/01(02)/College Council minutes; *Varsity*, 27 October, 3 November 1904.

15 For "Brute Force," see James A. Tucker, "In the Days of 'Moral Suasion,'" *Varsity*, 18 December 1900.

16 *Varsity*, 16 December 1903.

17 Hutton, "University Students in Oxford and Toronto," 209–10.

18 *Varsity*, 12 January 1912.

19 Ibid., 17 January, 17 December 1913.

20 Ibid., 1 February 1915.

21 Ibid., 17 March 1920.

22 Ibid., 16, 18 February 1921; 7, 9 March 1921.

23 Lit. minutes, 4 December 1934, UTA/A69-0011.

24 Lit. minutes, 25 September 1935.

25 *Varsity*, 9 December 1925.

26 Lit. minutes, 2 February 1938; *Varsity*, 3 February 1938.

27 See *Varsity*, 12, 17 February 1948; 12 October, 23 November 1949; 23 November, 8 December 1950; 24, 27 November 1952; 10 February 1956; Lit. minutes, 2 November 1949; 2 December 1952.

28 Lit. Executive minutes, 2 December 1930, UTA/A75-0013.

29 *Varsity*, 17–18 January 1940; Lit. minutes, 17 January 1940.

30 *Varsity*, 10 January, 20 February 1947.

31 See *Varsity*, 14 November 1952; 7, 14 February 1957; 7, 27 November 1957; Lit. minutes, 6 February 1957.

32 Lit. minutes, 10 October 1950.

33 Lit. minutes, 21 November 1950; *Varsity*, 22 November 1950.

34 *Varsity*, 21 November 1951.

35 Ibid., 21–22 October 1952.

36 Ibid., 18 December 1895.

37 Ibid., 26 January 1892.

38 Ibid., 18 December 1895.

39 Ibid., 22 January 1896.

40 Ibid., 22 October 1904.

41 "Constitution of the Grace Hall Memorial Library," in the WLS's *Constitution*; *Varsity*, 18 February 1903.
42 *Varsity*, 26 January 1909.
43 Ibid., 25 October 1911; 24 November 1913.
44 Ibid., 13 November 1914.
45 Ibid., 9 February 1917.
46 Ibid., 9, 23 November 1917.
47 Ibid., 24 January 1919.
48 Ibid., 25 February 1922.
49 *Report of the President of the University of Toronto* (1930/31), 11.
50 *Torontonensis* (1937): 249.
51 *Varsity*, 10 October 1923; 14 October 1948.
52 Ibid., 27 January 1927.
53 *Torontonensis* (1937): 249; *Torontonensis* (1939): 251.
54 College Council minutes, 18 March, 5 April 1946, UTA/A69-0016/02(02)/College Council minutes; *Varsity*, 3 March 1950.
55 *Varsity*, 15 November 1923.
56 Ibid., 1 November 1927. Reference to the "Gowns" issue can also be found in McKillop, *Matters of Mind*, 415.
57 *Varsity*, 23 November 1955.
58 Ibid., 1 December 1955; 6 January 1956.
59 For the role of teas and student opinion on them at universities in the United States, see Miller-Bernal, *Separate by Degree*, 121–2.
60 See *Varsity*, 16 November 1925; 9 March, 19 October 1926; 21 November 1928.
61 Ibid., 18 January 1952.
62 Ibid., 29 January 1954.
63 *Varsity*, 5 February 1954.
64 Ibid., 19 November 1946; 19 February 1947; College Council minutes, 10 January 1947.
65 *Varsity*, 23 November 1951.
66 Ibid., 9 October 1952.
67 Ibid., 25 November 1921.
68 See, for example, ibid., 30 November 1934.
69 Ibid., 14 January 1935.
70 Ibid., 30 November 1937.
71 Ibid., 19 January 1938; *Torontonensis* (1939): 256.
72 *Varsity*, 21 October 1943; 17 March 1944.
73 Ibid., 26, 29 November 1946.
74 *Varsity*, 2 February 1955.
75 Ibid., 7 October, 1 November 1955.

76 Ibid., 28 November 1957; 20, 24 January 1958.
77 Ibid., 20 February, 5 March 1958.
78 Owram, *Born at the Right Time*, 180–3.
79 *Varsity*, 23, 25 October 1963.
80 Ibid., 24 February 1965.
81 Ibid., 9 November 1962; *Gargoyle*, 9 February 1965.
82 *Gargoyle*, 9 December 1965.
83 Ibid., 20 January, 3 February 1966.
84 Ibid., 3, 24 November 1966; *Varsity*, 23 November 1966.
85 *Varsity*, 10 January 1967.
86 Ibid., 16 January 1967; Bissell, *Halfway up Parnassus*, 126.
87 *Varsity*, 13, 15, 17 February 1967.
88 The best description is in Rae, *From Protest to Power*, 31–2.
89 *Gargoyle*, 10 October, 21 November 1968.
90 *Varsity*, 25 November 1964.
91 Ibid., 2 December 1965.
92 Ibid., 22 September, 18 October 1967; *Gargoyle*, 26 September 1968; 30 January 1969.
93 *University of Toronto Act* (1947): sec. 70(2b)
94 *Gargoyle*, 4 November 1965; 3 February 1966.
95 *Varsity*, 29 November 1967; *Gargoyle*, 14 December 1967; 6 March 1968.
96 Douglas LePan to Claude Bissell, 15 April 1969, UTA/A77-0019/003.
97 *Varsity*, 26, 28 February 1964.
98 See ibid., 8 October 1965; *Gargoyle*, 10 March, 3 November 1966.
99 *Gargoyle*, 27 February 1970; 9 November 1971.
100 *Varsity*, 15 September 1972; *Gargoyle*, 22 November 1972.

CHAPTER TWO

1 Loudon, *Studies of Student Life*, vol. 5, 223; Wallace, "Background," 7. Wallace claimed that his statement followed from a "good deal of research," none of which has been preserved, as well as from his study of King's College graduates; see Wallace, "The Graduates of King's College, Toronto," 163–4.
2 Gaffield et al., "Student Populations and Graduate Careers," 7.
3 Keane, "Rediscovering Ontario University Students," table 9.2. Keane's geographical divisions were more detailed and do not exactly match the data codes used for this study. Keane, like Gaffield et al., made his calculations using place of residence, not place of birth.

4 Ibid., 871; Keane also disputes Wallace's claims for King's College, saying "only 25 per cent of the 96 known King's College entrants [for 1842–45] were from rural home residences or settlements of less than 200 persons," see "Rediscovering Ontario University Students," 655.

5 Westfall, "The Divinity 150 Project," 58–9.

6 Keane, "Rediscovering Ontario University Students," 851–2. It is unclear how such questions would be formulated.

7 For Toronto percentages, see Bloomfield, "Lawyers as Members of Urban Business Elites in Southern Ontario," 116.

8 Moore, *The Law Society of Upper Canada*, 79.

9 Gidney and Millar, *Professional Gentlemen*, 171.

10 Moore, *The Law Society of Upper Canada*, 88–9.

11 Ibid., 115.

12 Ibid., 106.

13 Gidney and Millar, *Professional Gentlemen*, 61–5, 312.

14 This figure may be slightly low, as it is possible some local reeveship may have escaped the notice of the sources consulted during the research.

15 Willie, "'It Is Every Man for Himself,'" 270, 277–8.

16 Moore, *The Law Society of Upper Canada*, 131–2.

17 Kyer and Bickenbach, *The Fiercest Debate*, 27–8.

18 Ibid., 31. King is mentioned in Moore, *The Law Society of Upper Canada*, 170.

19 Moore, *The Law Society of Upper Canada*, 155.

20 Various sources for these marriage connections exist. See especially Chadwick, *Ontarian Families*, vol. 1, 35, 117–9, 177; vol. 2, 45–7. For the Blakes, see Regehr, "Elite Relationships," 207–47.

21 Not all of these alliances can be directly attributed to the Lit. The interrelationship of the Cronyn and Blake families, for example, had been cemented during the journey of the *Anne of Halifax* from Ardagh, Ireland, to Upper Canada. See "Cronyn, Benjamin," *Dictionary of Canadian Biography*, vol. 10, 206.

22 Cole, "'A Learned and Honorable Body,'" 217–8, 224.

23 Williams, *Duff: A Life in the Law*.

24 *Globe*, 7 March 1876.

25 Gidney and Millar, *Professional Gentlemen*, 152–3.

26 For an example in the Anglican Church, see Westfall, "The Divinity 150 Project," 23–8.

27 Gidney and Millar, *Professional Gentlemen*, 133.

28 Ibid., 260–1, 276.

29 Hague, "The College History," 3–4.

30 Ibid., 5.
31 Ibid., 18–20.
32 Wallace, *A History of the University of Toronto*, 246–7.
33 Fraser, *Church, College, and Clergy*, 53–7.
34 Ibid., 78.
35 Wallace, *A History of the University of Toronto*, 244–5.
36 McNeill, *The Presbyterian Church in Canada*, 241.
37 Gauvreau, *Evangelical Century*, 152–4.
38 See Westfall, "The Divinity 150 Project," Ch. 1, 17.
39 "McLeod, Angus Jonas", *Dictionary of Canadian Biography*, Vol. XII, 670–1.
40 Gauvreau, *Evangelical Century*, 152–4, 202.
41 Allen, *The Social Passion*, 122, 274, 275. Not one of Allen's activist preachers was a member of a Lit. executive.
42 Airhart, *Serving the Present Age*, 52–3.
43 Westfall, "Divinity 150 Project," 17.
44 It must be noted, however, that Lewellys Barker does not mention the Lit. in his autobiography. See Barker, *Time and the Physician*, 25–36.
45 The Ontario high school system was created by act of provincial parliament in 1871. Some of the early officers of the Lit. taught at grammar schools, and are included in the category "high school level."
46 Gidney and Millar, *Professional Gentlemen*, 235–41.
47 Ibid., 244–5.
48 Gidney and Millar, *Inventing Secondary Education*, 269.
49 Wallace, *A History of the University of Toronto*, 112–3.
50 Loudon, *Sir William Mulock*, 45.
51 Inglis, *Northern Vagabond*.
52 Although geography was an interest of many in Canada by the late 1850s, it was not a program as such or a field recognized as separate. For instance, Henry Youle Hind, who participated in the Canadian Red River expedition of 1857, is generally described as a geologist and chemist; as well, Hind's university degrees were all honorary. The entire 1857 expedition was a collection of gifted amateurs, not professionals. See Morton, *Henry Youle Hind*, 1–57.
53 Bledstein, *The Culture of Professionalism*, 134–5, 288.

CHAPTER THREE

1 Two scholars have made attempts to define the characteristics of this student body. Keith Walden states that the University of

Toronto was attended by geographically and culturally disparate students who needed to be moulded into group cohesiveness by periodic initiation rituals. See also Walden, "Hazes, Hustles, Scraps and Stunts," 95–6, 111. A.B. McKillop, somewhat conversely, assumes that students at the university all shared a late-Victorian outlook on life; see McKillop, "Marching as to War," 75.

2 Axelrod, *Making a Middle Class*, 8–9, table 1.

3 McKillop, *Matters of Mind*, 163–70.

4 Axelrod, *Making a Middle Class*, 10.

5 The figures for five years after graduation, not shown in the tables, reveal sixteen white-collar workers.

6 Of the 613 University of Toronto students who died on active service during the First World War, 217 had at one point attended University College. One hundred and seventy-eight of them attended after 1908. One hundred and thiry-four former officers of the Lit. from the 1890–1916 period served during the war, all but ten as officers; fourteen made the supreme sacrifice. Among the pre-1890 officers of the Lit., few served, but one of them who did was Major-General Malcolm S. Mercer of the class of 1885, who died while commanding the Third Division of the Canadian army; see *University of Toronto Roll of Service, 1914–1918*.

7 The increase in university-trained engineers is accurately shown in Millard, *The Master Spirit of the Age*, 129, figure 7, table 7.

8 Cole, "'A Learned and Honorable Body,'" 69–72.

9 Moore, *The Law Society of Upper Canada*, 171.

10 *Varsity*, 13 February 1934.

11 Dawson, *William Lyon Mackenzie King*, 31.

12 Lit. minutes, 3 November 1893; 8 December 1893; 12 October 1894; 16 November 1894.

13 King briefly considered running for the Lit. elections in the spring of 1894, but ultimately decided not to in order to concentrate on his academic work. He did participate actively in behind-the-scenes organizing for those elections and also the ones held in 1895; see *Mackenzie King Diaries*, 27–8 February, 6 March 1894; 8 March 1895.

14 *Varsity*, 29 November 1955; see also 22 January 1924.

15 Graham, *Arthur Meighen*, 20–1.

16 Bell, "The Lit. 1854–1934," 24.

17 Lit. minutes, 26 October 1894. This dovetails nicely with Graham's assertion that Meighen remained bashful and unassuming as an undergraduate; see Graham, *Arthur Meighen*, 22.

18 Lit. minutes, 2 March 1895. In 1925, the *Varsity* reported of Meighen, "He was quiet and unassuming at College and was a brilliant mathematician." See "Varsity Men in Politics," *Varsity*, 28 October 1925.

19 Graham, *Arthur Meighen*, 44.

20 Public Archives of Ontario (PAO)/George S. Henry Family Papers/George S. Henry Scrapbooks/File F-9-5-0-7/University of Toronto material, 1895–99.

21 *Varsity*, 17 March 1891. Ferguson's biographers missed this key event in the life of a political animal.

22 Maurice Hutton used those exact words in supporting Stuart's application for a fellowship in political science, adding, "his drive and energy are likely to make him to the end a leader in both the practical and the intellectual world." Hutton to the Minister of Education, February 1891, PAO/RG-2-29-2-56/Ministry of Education/University of Toronto Application Files/Stuart, Charles Allen.

23 McGregor Young, "The University and the Legal Profession," *Varsity*, 21 October 1902.

24 Moore, *The Law Society of Upper Canada*, 164, 225. Craig McKay's election leaflet for 1941 is reprinted in Moore, but his name does not appear in the index.

25 Bloomfield, "Lawyers as Members of Urban Business Elites," 134–9.

26 See Gunn, "The Lawyer as Entrepreneur," 235–62.

27 Moore, *The Law Society of Upper Canada*, 208.

28 Ibid., 209.

29 Gelman, "The 'Feminization' of the High School," 78.

30 Ibid., 82.

31 Professor William Dale was dismissed by the University of Toronto in 1895 for inflammatory remarks on the credentials of newly promoted Professer George Wrong; see Friedland, *University of Toronto*, 166.

32 For the activities of this faction, see McKillop, *Contours of Canadian Thought*, 82–91.

33 Horn, *Academic Freedom in Canada*, 55–60; see also Gingras, *Physics and the Rise of Scientific Research*, 46.

34 McKillop, *Contours of Canadian Thought*, 93.

35 Ibid., 94–5. For Falconer, see Greenlee, *Sir Robert Falconer*, 150–1.

36 Jarrell, *The Cold Light of Dawn*, 127, 195–6.

37 Ibid., 87–110, 127–9. Robert Motherwell, Ralph DeLury, and John B. Cannon's loss of equipment is detailed on 104.

38 Gingras, *Physics*, 99–102.

39 Richard Jarrell seems to have been willing to consider that the Literary and Scientific Society might have been "strong competition" for the Toronto Astronomical Society (TAS) and thus a reason why no members of the TAS were from the University of Toronto. This is, of course, completely ludicrous. See Jarrell, *Cold Light of Dawn*, 79.

40 Gingras, *Physics and the Rise of Scientific Research*, 73. Eli Burton supervised the construction of the first electron microscope in North America. It is currently on display in the Ontario Science Centre's Hall of Technology.

41 This thesis has recently been challenged; see White, *Gentlemen Engineers*, 181–8.

42 Gidney and Millar, *Professional Gentlemen*, 228–9. For Adam Crooks' involvement, see Young, *Early Engineering Education*, 46–55. For a contradictory view of this process, see White, "Professionals and Academics."

43 Young, *Early Engineering Education*, 82.

44 Millard, *The Master Spirit of the Age*, 31–3, 40, 69.

45 Gidney and Millar, *Professional Gentlemen*, 227, 231–2.

46 Richard Allen's book on the "social gospel" was published after many of them had died; obituaries therefore did not mention any connection with any purported social movements. Even so, one would have expected that more of these university-trained clerics would have been attuned to social issues and have conducted themselves accordingly.

47 Grant, *The Church in the Canadian Era*, 128

48 Clifford, *The Resistance to Church Union in Canada*, 236–7.

49 American Institute of Actuaries, *The Record* (1930). Actuarial Society of America, *Yearbook* (1908), (1930). The two groups amalgamated in 1949 to form the Society of Actuaries; see Society of Actuaries, *Transactions* (1949).

50 Obituary of Charles Henry Armstrong, Society of Actuaries, *Transactions* 5 (1953), 379. The records of the Actuaries Club of Toronto have not yet been located.

51 Sibbald, "The Civil Service as a Career for a University Graduate," 166–7.

52 Ibid., 169–70.

53 Ibid., 172.

54 Humphries, *"Honest Enough to be Bold"*, 91.

CHAPTER FOUR

1 LaPierre, "The Academic Life of Canadian Coeds," 307.

2 LaPierre, "The First Generation," 17.

3 Marks and Gaffield, "Women at Queen's University," 336–46.
4 Fingard, "College, Career, and Community," 26–50.
5 Marks and Gaffield, "Women at Queen's University," 338–9.
6 Fingard, "College, Career, and Community," 27, 34.
7 Ibid., 34
8 Marks and Gaffield, "Women at Queen's University," 338–9.
9 Ibid., 335–6.
10 McPherson, "Careers of Canadian University Women," 4.
11 Massey, *Occupations for Trained Women in Canada*, 12.
12 Marks and Gaffield, "Women at Queen's University," 340–1. Unlike Marks and Gaffield, I do not combine the "manager, civil servant, agent" category with "professionals"; this difference accounts for the slight disparity in our findings.
13 LaPierre, "The Academic Life of Canadian Coeds," 307.
14 *The University of Toronto Song Book*, 23–4. The song was sung at the annual dinner of University College, 9 December 1888; see UTA/B65-0038/002. Similar verses existed at the University of British Columbia during the 1920s; see Stewart, *"It's Up to You"*, 126.
15 Quoted in Stamp, "Teaching Girls their 'God Given Place in Life,'" 28.
16 Fingard, "College, Career, and Community," 31, 41.
17 Marks and Gaffield, "Women at Queen's University," 343.
18 McPherson, "Careers of Canadian University Women," 41.
19 Ray, "What Becomes of the University Woman," 95.
20 See "After Forty Years," and "Those Forty Years, 1903–1943." The figures are eleven of twenty married for 1902 and twelve of twenty for 1903.
21 Gaffield and Marks, "Women at Queen's University," 343, 349fn36.
22 Fingard, "College, Career, and Community," 32, 36–8, 44. For contrast, see LaPierre, "The First Generation," 248–50.
23 Ray, "What Becomes of the University Woman?," 96.
24 Ray, "What Becomes of the University Woman?, Part II," 125–6.
25 Kinnear, *Margaret McWilliams*, 35–6.
26 Ibid., 38–9.
27 Nett, *Canadian Families*, 139. Nett's table implies this would hold for the ten to twenty years previous when the majority of the WLS/WUA officers would have reached child-bearing age.
28 Ibid., 145. Nett's choice of data in this book is very idiosyncratic.
29 In Australia, the connection between higher education and a declining birth rate was the focus of a Commission of Enquiry

in 1903; see Mackinnon, "Interfering with Nature's Mandate," 219–38. Similar arguments were made in the United States; see Miller-Bernal, *Separate by Degree*, 65–66. No Canadian contribution to the debate has yet been located.

30 McPherson, "Careers of Canadian University Women," 19A.
31 Gaffield and Marks, "Women at Queen's University," 345.
32 For women and the law, see Moore, *The Law Society of Upper Canada*, 180–4, 202–3.
33 McPherson, "Careers of Canadian University Women," 4
34 LaPierre, "The First Generation," 252.
35 Gelman, "The 'Feminization' of the High School," 85.
36 Ibid., 84.
37 Gelman, "Women Secondary School Teachers," 259.
38 Ray, "What Becomes of the University Woman?", 96.
39 Lanning, *The National Album*, 149.
40 Ibid., 150–2.
41 LaPierre, "The First Generation," 270–2.
42 *Annual Report of the University College Alumnae Association*, 1906/07, UTA/P79-0264. The minutes of the association are located in UTA/A69-0011/13–4.
43 LaPierre, "The First Generation," 274.
44 Prentice et. al., *Canadian Women*, 192. This source says the League was founded in 1912.
45 Baldwin Room, Metro Central Reference Library/History of Canadian Settlements, file S-54.
46 James, "Gender, Class, and Ethnicity," 174.
47 Central Neighbourhood House Yearbooks (1912, 1913), City of Toronto Archives/SC5/Central Neighbourhood House/Box 19.
48 See, for example, Gagan, *A Sensitive Independence*; Rutherdale, "Models of Grace and Boundaries of Culture."
49 *Torontonensis* (1908), 300; *Torontonensis* (1909), 316; *Torontonensis* (1911), 325. See also James,"Gender, Class, and Ethnicity." 65, n138. The actual number of students from University College who participated in the settlement movement is not known.
50 Lanning, *The National Album*, 163–6.
51 For the list of notable women, see *Seventy-Five Years of CFUW*, 115–28.

CHAPTER FIVE

1 *President's Report* (1947/8): 5.
2 Axelrod, *Making a Middle Class*, 29–30.

3 Drummond, *Progress Without Planning*, 364.
4 *President's Report* (1926/7): 11–12.
5 Axelrod, *Making a Middle Class*, 32–4.
6 *Varsity*, 19 October 1931.
7 McGillicuddy, *Between Lectures*, 28.
8 Moore, *The Law Society of Upper Canada*, 217.
9 *Varsity*, 25 January 1952. Lit. minutes, 5 February 1952.
10 This is especially so since the possibilities of elevation to the bench for this group had not yet been exhausted.
11 For the tension between the Law Society and accountancy, see Moore, *The Law Society of Upper Canada*, 247, 272.
12 Ibid., 196.
13 Ibid., 255–6.
14 Creighton, *A Sum of Yesterdays*, 100–10.
15 McKillop, *Matters of Mind*, 332–3.
16 Creighton, *Sum of Yesterdays*, 154–8.
17 *Checkmark*, December 1961.
18 Ibid., February 1962.
19 Creighton, *Sum of Yesterdays*, 284–90.
20 *The Story of the Firm: Clarkson, Gordon and Co., 1864–1964*, 81–148.
21 Dunstall, *The Story of the Life Underwriters Association*, 16.
22 Ibid., 65–6.
23 Ibid., 65.
24 Ibid., 70–1.
25 Axelrod, *Making a Middle Class*, 121–4.
26 *Varsity*, 30 October 1951.
27 Ibid., 1 November 1922.
28 Ibid., 11 November 1937; 27–8 November 1940.
29 Ibid., 7 February 1950.
30 Morris, *The Film Companion*, 24–5, 78–81.
31 Ibid., 249–50, 318–9. Rasky states in his autobiography, "As soon as I attended the University of Toronto, I quickly registered at the *Varsity* paper and became involved in the UC Follies, the annual college variety show." The Lit. is not mentioned at all. See Rasky, *Nobody Swings on Sunday*, 79.
32 Jones, *The Best Butler in the Business*, 6–12. Jones mentions Daly's involvement as producer of the University College *Follies* and his membership on the Hart House Art Committee, but does not mention the Lit.
33 *Varsity*, 11 January 1928.
34 McNaught and Stephenson, *The Story of Advertising in Canada*, 261.

35 Paul Bridle wrote Claude Bissell years later and told him that "Saul's being in the Department had something to do with my joining." See Bridle to Bissell, 18 September 1961, UTA/B84-0036/006; see also Harris, "At Home Abroad," 131–3.
36 Hodgetts et al., *The Biography of an Institution*, 96–9.
37 Ibid., 439.
38 Axelrod, *Making a Middle Class*, 50.
39 Ibid., 60–1.

CHAPTER SIX

1 Stewart, *"It's up to you,"* 97–9.
2 This point is made with reference especially to Jewish women in Marks, "Kale Meydelach or Shulamith Girls," 299–300.
3 Stewart, *"It's up to you,"* 97–9.
4 Ibid., 105.
5 McKillop, *Matters of Mind*, 424–5.
6 The information on women in education for this period is not as precise as it should be.
7 The institutional barriers against women in the professoriate are further documented in Fingard, "Gender and Inequality at Dalhousie" and Kinnear, "Disappointment in Discourse."
8 Wright, "The Importance of Being Sexist," 19.
9 Moore, *The Law Society of Upper Canada*, 268–9.
10 Burke, *Seeking the Highest Good*, 100–14.
11 For a discussion of other professions such as nursing and accountancy, see Smyth et al., *Challenging Professions*.
12 Strong-Boag, *The New Day Recalled*, 83.
13 Ibid.
14 Nett, *Canadian Families*, 139.
15 In 1998 the database listed 274 married women and 469 children from this cohort. Since that point, fourteen marriages and nearly one hundred more children have been confirmed.
16 Strong-Boag, *The New Day Recalled*, 95.
17 McKillop, *Matters of Mind*, 555–6.
18 Ibid., 567–8.
19 Prentice et al., *Canadian Women*, 324.
20 Francis, *Frank H. Underhill*, 36.
21 McKillop, *Matters of Mind*, 423.
22 Gillett, *We Walked Very Warily*, 237.
23 *McGill Daily*, 24–5 January 1949.
24 See chapter 1.
25 Axelrod, *Making a Middle Class*, 108.

26 See King, "Centres of 'Home-Like Influence'", 39–59.
27 Prentice et al., 316.
28 For examples of this, see ibid., 243–4, 308.
29 See, for example, the Queen's student of 1928 quoted in Prentice et al., 261.

CHAPTER SEVEN

1 *Globe and Mail,* 3 December 1997.
2 *Toronto Star,* 7 September 1998.
3 Owram, *Born at the Right Time,* 210–5, 293.
4 *Varsity,* 6 October 1967.
5 Ibid., 27 September, 6 October 1971.
6 Support for the differing experience of the sons and daughters of recent immigrants is provided in Anisef et al., *Opportunity and Uncertainty,* 256.
7 Axelrod, *Scholars and Dollars,* 28.
8 *Gargoyle,* 25 November 1965.
9 *Varsity,* 26 November 1965.
10 Ibid., 29 January 1968.
11 Owram, *Born at the Right Time,* 269–70.
12 During the research process, other scholars have pointed out that at least two earlier officers of the Lit. are now widely suspected of having been homosexual. Because neither officially "came out" and because I have no political or scholarly interest in "outing" them, these cases have been filed under "unwarranted speculation."
13 Harvey, *Education and Employment of Arts and Science Graduates,* 99.
14 Harvey's categories are especially poor for comparing the number of graduates entering the professions. He notes that 6.3% entered the "manufacturing industry," 4.5% "trade," and 15.3% "service," but nowhere defines what these categories mean; see ibid., 306–7.
15 Ibid., 254.
16 Kushner et al., *The Market Situation for University Graduates,* 23.
17 Axelrod, *Scholars and Dollars,* 143–5.
18 For more on these issues in the 1970s and 1980s, see Anisef et al., *Opportunity and Uncertainty.*

APPENDIX A

1 Brown, "How the J.C.R. Became Gilt-Edged," 10. See also UTA/A75-0013/University College/minutes of Lit. executive meeting, 28 September 1926.

2 This tradition was briefly revived in 1999 to honour Winnie Wong, the first female speaker of the Lit. She appears as "Ms. W. Wong."

3 The taxonomy of student memorials at universities ranges from the "vittores" scribbled by successful students on the walls of the University of Salamanca, through the academic honours such as the Bronze Tablets at the University of Illinois, the war memorials at many Canadian universities, and the two wooden tablets honouring the presidents of the Alma Mater Society and Graduate Student Society at Queen's. No example to date has been found, however, of another series of walls listing the entire executives of a student organization, placed on the walls by the organization itself, to honour only the election of those students to office.

APPENDIX B

1 Johnson, *Becoming Prominent*.
2 Ibid., 4.
3 Axelrod, *Making a Middle Class*, 174–7.

Select Bibliography

ARCHIVAL SOURCES

Baldwin Room, Toronto Central Reference Library

S54 – History of Canadian Settlements.

City of Toronto Archives

SC5 – Central Neighbourhood House.
SC24 – University Settlement House.

Law Society of Upper Canada

Barristers Records.
Barristers Green Cards.
Barristers White Cards.
Ontario Barristers Biographical Research Project (OBBRP).
Rolls of Members.

National Archives of Canada

MC30D262/Owen McGillicuddy Papers.
MG30D319/10–19/David Reid Keys Papers.

Provincial Archives of Ontario

RG-2-29-2/Ministry of Education/University of Toronto Faculty Application Files.
RG-2-114-1/Ministry of Education/Superannuation Application Files.
RG-80-2/Records of the Office of the Registrar General/Births 1869–1900.
RG-80-5/Records of the Office of the Registrar General/Marriages 1869–1915.
RG-80-8/Records of the Office of the Registrar General/Deaths 1869–1925.
RG-80-27/Toronto City Marriage Register.
George S. Henry Family Papers.
1871 Census Records.

Fred J. Reynolds Genealogical Collection, Fort Wayne, Indiana

Soundex Index to the 1880 United States Census.
Soundex Index to the 1900 United States Census.
Soundex Index to the 1920 United States Census.
United States City Directory Collection.
United States Census, 1880, 1900, 1920

University College Alumni Association

Alumni Record Cards.
WUA Historical File.

University of Toronto Archives

A65-0014/Langton Family.
A67-0007/Office of the President.
A69-0008/48–83/Faculty of Arts Admissions Files, 1905–1921.
A69-0008/208–210/Physical and Health Education Admissions Files.
A69-0011/University College.
A69-0016/College Council Minutes.
A71-0008, roll 11/SPS Students Registry.
A72-0024/Department of Alumni Affairs.
A73-0026/Graduate Records Department.
A74-0008, box 10/Dean Young Historical Research Notes.
A74-0011/Dean of Women, University College.
A74-0027/Department of Astronomy.

A75-0013/Literary and Athletic Society Executive Minutes.
A77-0019/Office of the President.
A89-0011/Student Records of the Faculty of Arts.
A1999-003/Library.
B65-0038/Ethelbert Lincoln Hill.
B84-0036/Claude Thomas Bissell.
"Clegg-Johnson Files."
Acta Victoriana, 1878–   .
Alumni Bulletin, 1943–1955.
Arbor, 1910–1913.
College Topics, 1898–1901.
Gargoyle, 1954–1973.
Sesame, 1897–1901.
Torontonensis, 1898–1968.
University College Alumnae Association Report, 1908/09.
University College Calendar, 1857–1886
University College Literary and Athletic Society. *Constitution and By-Laws*, 1923–46.
University College Literary and Scientific Society. *Constitution and By-Laws*, 1857–1910.
University College Undergraduate, 1932–68.
University of Toronto Calendar, 1887–1973.
University of Toronto Monthly, 1900–47.
University of Toronto. *President's Reports*, 1906–71.
Varsity, 1880–1973.
Varsity Graduate, 1948–67.

OTHER SOURCES

Actuarial Society of America. *Yearbook*. New York, 1911–1949.
Airhart, Phyllis D. *Serving the Present Age: Revivalism, Progressivism, and the Methodist Tradition in Canada*. Montreal: McGill-Queen's University Press, 1992.
Alexander, W.J., ed. *The University of Toronto and Its Colleges 1827–1906*. Toronto: The University Librarian, 1906.
Allen, Richard. *The Social Passion: Religious and Social Reform in Canada, 1914–1928*. Toronto: University of Toronto Press, 1973.
Allmendiger, David F., Jr. *Paupers and Scholars: The Transformation of Student Life in Nineteenth-Century New England* New York: St. Martin's Press, 1975.
American Institute of Actuaries. *The Record*. Chicago, 1909–1949.
Anisef, Paul, et al. *Opportunity and Uncertainty: Life Course Experiences of the Class of '73*. Toronto: University of Toronto Press, 2000.

Axelrod, Paul. *Making a Middle Class: Student Life in English Canada During the Thirties*. Montreal: McGill-Queen's University Press, 1990.

– *Scholars and Dollars: Politics, Economics, and the Universities of Ontario, 1945–1980*. Toronto: University of Toronto Press, 1982.

Axelrod, Paul, and John G. Reid. *Youth, University, and Canadian Society: Essays in the Social History of Higher Education*. Montreal: McGill-Queen's University Press, 1989.

Bailey, Thomas M., ed. *Dictionary of Hamilton Biography*. Hamilton: Dictionary of Hamilton Biography, 1981– .

Barker, Lewellys F. *Time and the Physician*. New York: G.P. Putnam's Sons, 1942.

Bell, Richard A. "The Lit, 1854–1934." *University College Undergraduate* 4 (1934): 16–29.

Bissell, Claude. *Halfway up Parnassus: A Personal Account of the University of Toronto, 1932–1971*. Toronto: University of Toronto Press, 1974.

– *The Strength of the University*. Toronto: University of Toronto Press, 1968.

– ed. *University College: A Portrait*. Toronto: University of Toronto Press, 1953.

Bledstein, Burton J. *The Culture of Professionalism: The Middle Class and the Development of Higher Education in America*. New York: W.W. Norton and Company, 1976.

Bloomfield, Elizabeth. "Lawyers as Members of Urban Business Elites in Southern Ontario." In *Beyond the Law: Lawyers and Business in Canada, 1830 to 1930*, edited by Carol Wilton. Toronto: The Osgoode Society, 1990.

Brown, Egerton. "How the J.C.R. Became Gilt-Edged." *University College Magazine* 12, 1 (1988): 10.

Brown, Harold E. *University of Toronto Memorial Book, 1939–1945*. Toronto: Soldiers' Tower Committee, University of Toronto, 1994.

Burke, Colin B. *American Collegiate Populations: A Test of the Traditional View*. New York: New York University Press, 1982.

Burke, Sarah Z. *Seeking the Highest Good: Social Service and Gender and the University of Toronto, 1888–1937*. Toronto: University of Toronto Press, 1996.

Canadian Law List. Toronto: Canadian Legal Publishing Co., 1901–42 and Canada Law Book Co., 1960–99.

Canadian Legal Directory. Toronto: Canada Legal Directory Co., 1911–99.

Canadian Who's Who. Toronto: University of Toronto Press, 1910– .

Chadwick, Edward M. *Ontarian Families*. 2 vols. Lambertville, NJ: Hunterdon House, 1970.

Church of England in Canada Yearbook. Toronto, 1919–90.

Clifford, N. Keith. *The Resistance to Church Union in Canada*. Vancouver: UBC Press, 1985.

Cole, Curtis. "'A Learned and Honorable Body': The Professionalization of the Ontario Bar, 1867–1929." PhD diss. University of Western Ontario, 1987.

Collard, Edgar, ed. *The McGill You Knew*. Don Mills, ON: Longman, 1975.

College of Physicians and Surgeons of Ontario. *Ontario Medical Register*. Hamilton, 1898.

Coutts, James. *A History of the University of Glasgow*. Glasgow: James Maclehouse and Sons, 1909.

Craick, William Arnot. *The Annals of Nineteen-Two*. Toronto: University of Toronto Class of 1902, 1952.

Creighton, Philip. *A Sum of Yesterdays: Being a History of the First One Hundred Years of the Institute of Chartered Accountants of Ontario*. Toronto: The Institute of Chartered Accountants of Ontario, 1984.

Crockford's Clerical Directory. London, 1872–1982.

Dawson, R. McGregor. *William Lyon Mackenzie King: A Political Biography, 1874–1923*. Toronto: University of Toronto Press, 1958.

Dictionary of Canadian Biography. 14 vols. Toronto: University of Toronto Press, 1966–   .

Directory of Canadian Chartered Accountants. Toronto: Canadian Institute of Chartered Accountants, 1949–85.

Drummond, Ian M. *Progress Without Planning: The Economic History of Ontario from Confederation to the Second World War*. Toronto: University of Toronto Press, 1987.

Dunstall, Leslie W. *The Story of the Life Underwriters Association of Canada, 1906–1956*. Canada: The Life Underwriters of Canada, 1956.

Evans, Ralph, ed. *A Register of Rhodes Scholars, 1903–1995*. Oxford: Rhodes Trust, 1996.

Evans, Margaret A. *Sir Oliver Mowat*. Toronto: University of Toronto Press, 1992.

Fairclough, Henry Rushton. *Warming Both Hands: The Autobiography of Henry Rushton Fairclough*. Stanford, CA: Stanford University Press, 1941.

Fingard, Judith "College, Career, and Community: Dalhousie Coeds 1881–1921." In *Youth, University, and Canadian Society: Essays in the Social History of Higher Education*, edited by Paul Axelrod and John G. Reid. Montreal: McGill-Queen's University Press, 1989.

– "Gender and Inequality at Dalhousie: Faculty Women before 1950." *Dalhousie Review* 64 (1984/85): 687–703.

Ford, Anne Rochon. *A Path Not Strewn with Roses: One Hundred Years of Women at the University of Toronto*. Toronto: University of Toronto Press, 1985.

Francis, R. Douglas. *Frank H. Underhill: Intellectual Provacateur*. Toronto: University of Toronto Press, 1986.

Fraser, Brian J. *Church, College, and Clergy: A History of Theological Education at Knox College, Toronto, 1844–1994*. Montreal: McGill-Queen's University Press, 1995.

Friedland, Martin. *The University of Toronto: A History*. Toronto: University of Toronto Press, 2002.

Frost, Stanley B. *McGill University: For the Advancement of Learning*. 2 vols. Montreal: McGill-Queen's University Press, 1980–84.

Gaffield, Chad, et al. "Student Populations and Graduate Careers: Queen's University, 1895–1900." In *Youth, University, and Canadian Society: Essays in the Social History of Higher Education*, edited by Paul Axelrod and John G. Reid. Montreal: McGill-Queen's University Press, 1989.

Gagan, Rosemary. *A Sensitive Independence: Canadian Methodist Women Missionaries in Canada and the Orient, 1881–1925*. Montreal: McGill-Queen's University Press, 1992.

Gauvreau, Michael. *Evangelical Century: College and Creed in English Canada from the Great Revival to the Great Depression*. Montreal: McGill-Queen's University Press, 1991.

Gelman, Susan. "The 'Feminization' of the High School: Women Secondary School Teachers in Toronto: 1871–1930." In *Gender and Education in Ontario: A Historical Reader*, edited by Ruby Heap and Alison Prentice. Toronto: Canadian Scholars' Press, 1991.

– "Women Secondary School Teachers: Ontario 1871–1930." PhD diss. University of Toronto, 1994.

Gidney, R.D., and W.P.J. Millar. *Inventing Secondary Education: The Rise of the High School in Nineteeneth-Century Ontario*. Montreal: McGill-Queen's University Press, 1990.

– *Professional Gentlemen: The Professions in Nineteenth-Century Ontario*. Toronto: University of Toronto Press, 1994.

Gillett, Margaret. *We Walked Very Warily: A History of Women at McGill*. Montreal: Eden Press, 1981.

Gingras, Yves. *Physics and the Rise of Scientific Research in Canada*. Montreal: McGill-Queen's University Press, 1991.

Graham, Roger. *Arthur Meighen: The Door of Opportunity*. Toronto: Clark Irwin and Company, 1960.

Grant, John Webster. *The Church in the Canadian Era*. 2nd ed. Burlington, ON: Welch Publishing, 1988.

Greenlee, James G. *Sir Robert Falconer: A Biography*. Toronto: University of Toronto Press, 1988.

Gunn, James H. "The Lawyer as Entrepreneur: Robert Home Smith in Early-Twentieth Century Toronto." In *Beyond the Law: Lawyers and Business in Canada 1830 to 1930*, edited by Carol Wilton. Toronto: The Osgoode Society, 1990.

Harding, Thomas S. *College Literary Societies: Their Contribution to Higher Education in the United States, 1815–1876*. New York: Pageant Press International, 1971.

Harris, R.S. "At Home Abroad: Varsity Graduates in External Affairs." *Varsity Graduate* 6 (1958): 131–3.

Harrison, Brian, ed. *The History of the University of Oxford*. Vol. 8. Oxford: The Clarendon Press, 1994.

Harvey, Edward B. *Education and Employment of Arts and Science Graduates: The Last Decade in Ontario*. Toronto: W. Kinmond, 1972.

Hague, Dyson. "The College History." In *The Jubilee Volume of Wycliffe College*. Toronto: Wycliffe College, 1927.

Heap, Ruby, and Alison Prentice. *Gender and Education in Ontario: A Historical Reader*. Toronto: Canadian Scholars' Press, 1991.

Hebrew University of Jerusalem Family Who's Who. Montreal: Wallace Press, 1969.

Hodgetts, J.E. et al., *The Biography of an Institution: The Civil Service Commission of Canada, 1908–1967*. Montreal: McGill-Queen's University Press, 1972.

Hodgins, John G. *Documentary History of Education in Upper Canada*. Vol. 14. Toronto: L.K. Cameron, 1906.

Hollis, Christopher. *The Oxford Union*, London: Evans Brothers, 1965.

Honour Classics in the University of Toronto. Toronto: University of Toronto Press, 1929.

Horn, D.B. *A Short History of the University of Edinburgh, 1556–1889*. Edinburgh: Edinburgh University Press, 1967.

Horn, Michiel. *Academic Freedom in Canada: A History*, Toronto: University of Toronto Press, 1999.

Horowitz, Helen Lefkowitz. *Campus Life: Undergraduate Cultures from the End of the Eighteenth Century to the Present*. New York: Alfred A. Knopf, 1987.

Humphries, Charles W. *"Honest Enough to be Bold": The Life and Times of Sir James Pliny Whitney*. Toronto: University of Toronto Press, 1985.

Hutton, Maurice. "University Students in Oxford and Toronto." *University of Toronto Monthly* 7 (1906/07): 205–12.

In Memory of Rev. James Ballantyne B.A. D.D., 1857–1921. Toronto: The Ryerson Press, 1922.

Inglis, Alex. *Northern Vagabond: The Life and Career of J.B. Tyrrell*. Toronto: McClelland and Stewart, 1978.

Institute of Chartered Accounts of Ontario. *Checkmark*. Toronto, 1959–95.

James, Cathy Leigh. "Gender, Class and Ethnicity in the Organization of Neighbourhood and Nation: The Role of Toronto's Settlement Houses in the Formation of the Canadian State, 1902–1914," PhD diss. University of Toronto, 1997.

Jarrell, Richard A. *The Cold Light of Dawn: A History of Canadian Astronomy*. Toronto: University of Toronto Press, 1988.

Jasen, Patricia. "'In Pursuit of Human Values (or Laugh When You Say That)': The Student Critique of the Arts Curriculum in the 1960s." In *Youth, University, and Canadian Society: Essays in the Social History of Higher Education*, edited by Paul Axelrod and John G. Reid. Montreal: McGill-Queen's University Press, 1989.

Johnson, J.K. *Becoming Prominent: Regional Leadership in Upper Canada, 1791–1841*. Kingston: McGill-Queen's University Press, 1989.

– ed. *Canadian Directory of Parliament, 1867–1967*. Ottawa: Queen's Printer, 1968.

Jones, D.B. *The Best Butler in the Business: Tom Daly of the National Film Board of Canada*. Toronto: University of Toronto Press, 1996.

The Jubilee Volume of Wycliffe College. Toronto: Wycliffe College, 1927.

Keane, David Ross. "Rediscovering Ontario University Students in the Mid-Nineteenth Century." PhD diss. University of Toronto, 1981.

Kimmel, David. "The People v. Margaret and Barker Fairley: The Waldorf Incident, 1949." Paper presented at the University College Symposium 20: Gossip, Denunciation and Praise, Toronto, January 1998.

King, Alison E. "'Centres of "Home-Like Influence"': Residences for Women at the University of Toronto." *Material History Review* 49 (1999): 39–59.

King, William Lyon Mackenzie. *Mackenzie King Diaries, 1893–1931*. Toronto: University of Toronto Press, 1973.

Kinnear, Mary. "Disappointment in Discourse: Women University Professors at the University of Manitoba Before 1970." *Historical Studies in Education* 4 (1992): 269–87.

– *Margaret McWilliams: Interwar Feminist*. Montreal: McGill-Queen's Univerisity Press, 1991.

Kushner, J., et al. *The Market Situation for University Graduates: Canada*. Ottawa: Research Branch, Program Development Service, Department of Manpower and Immigration Canada, 1971.

Kyer, C. Ian, and Jerome E. Bickenbach. *The Fiercest Debate: Cecil A. Wright, the Benchers, and Legal Education in Ontario, 1923–1957*. Toronto: University of Toronto Press, 1987.

Lanning, Robert. *The National Album: Collective Biography and the Formation of the Canadian Middle Class*. Ottawa: Carleton University Press, 1996.

LaPierre, Jo. "The Academic Life of Canadian Coeds, 1880–1900." In *Gender and Education in Ontario: A Historical Reader*, edited by Ruby Heap and Alison Prentice. Toronto: Canadian Scholars' Press, 1991.

LaPierre, Paula J.S. "The First Generation: The Experience of Women University Students in Central Canada." PhD diss. University of Toronto, 1993.

Levi, Charles. *The SAC Historical Project, 1930–1950*. Toronto, 1990. Self-published.

Loudon, William James. *Sir William Mulock: A Short Biography*. Toronto: Macmillian, 1932.

– *Studies of Student Life*. 8 vols. Toronto: Macmillan, 1923–4.

MacKay, W.A. *Zorra Boys at Home and Abroad: Or How to Succeed*. Toronto: William Briggs, 1900.

Mackinnon, Alison. "Interfering with Nature's Mandate: Women, Higher Education and Demographic Change." *Historical Studies in Education* 1 (1989): 219–38.

Mallet, Charles Edward. *A History of the University of Oxford*. Vol. 3. London: Methuen and Company, 1927.

Manitoba Library Association. *Pioneers and Early Citizens of Manitoba: A Dictionary of Manitoba Biography from the Earliest Times to 1920*. Winnipeg: Peguis Publishers, 1971.

Marks, Lynn. "Kale Meydelach or Shulamith Girls: Cultural Change and Continuity Among Jewish Parents and Daughters – A Case Study of Toronto's Harbord Collegiate Institute in the 1920s." In *Gender and Education in Ontario: A Historical Reader*, edited by Ruby Heap and Alison Prentice. Toronto: Canadian Scholars' Press, 1991.

Marks, Lynn and Chad Gaffield. "Women at Queen's University, 1895–1905: A 'Little Sphere' All Their Own." *Ontario History* 78 (1986): 331–49.

Martindale-Hubbell Canadian Law Directory. New Providence, NJ: Martindale-Hubbell, 1993.

Massey, Alice. *Occupations for Trained Women in Canada.* Toronto: J.M. Dent and Sons, 1920.

Masters, D.C. *Henry John Cody: An Outstanding Life.* Toronto: Dundurn Press, 1995.

McDowell, R.B. and D.A. Webb. *Trinity College Dublin, 1592–1952: An Academic History.* Cambridge: Cambridge University Press, 1982.

McGillicuddy, Paul Clark. *Between Lectures.* Toronto: Age Publications, 1939.

McKillop, A.B. *Contours of Canadian Thought.* Toronto: University of Toronto Press, 1987.

– "Marching as to War: Elements of Ontario Undergraduate Culture, 1880–1914." In *Youth, University, and Canadian Society: Essays in the Social History of Higher Education*, edited by Paul Axelrod and John G. Reid. Montreal: McGill-Queen's University Press, 1989.

– *Matters of Mind: The University in Ontario, 1791–1951,* Toronto: University of Toronto Press, 1994.

McLachlan, James. "The Choice of Hercules: American Student Societies in the Early 19th Century." In *The University in Society*, Vol. 2, edited by Lawrence Stone. Princeton: Princeton University Press, 1974.

McNaught, Carlton, and Harold E. Stephenson. *The Story of Advertising in Canada: A Chronicle of Fifty Years.* Toronto: The Ryerson Press, 1940.

McNeill, John Thomas. *The Presbyterian Church in Canada, 1875–1925.* Toronto: General Board of the Presbyterian Church in Canada, 1925.

McPherson, Elsinore. "Careers of Canadian University Women." Master's thesis, University of Toronto, 1920.

Meenan, James, ed. *Centenary History of the Literary and Historical Society of University College Dublin, 1855–1955.* Tralee, Ireland: Kerryman, 1956.

Millard, J. Rodney. *The Master Spirit of the Age: Canadian Engineers and the Politics of Professionalism.* Toronto: University of Toronto Press, 1988.

Miller-Bernal, Leslie. *Separate by Degree: Women Students' Experiences in Single-Sex and Coeducational Colleges.* New York: Peter Lang, 2000.

Montagnes, Ian. *Uncommon Fellowship: The Story of Hart House*. Toronto: University of Toronto Press, 1969.

Moore, Christopher. *The Law Society of Upper Canada and Ontario's Lawyers, 1797–1997*. Toronto: University of Toronto Press, 1997.

Morgan, Henry J. *The Canadian Men and Women of the Time*. Toronto, W. Briggs, 1898, 1912.

Morris, Peter. *The Film Companion*. Toronto: Irwin Publishing, 1984.

Morton, W.L. *Henry Youle Hind, 1823–1908*. Toronto: University of Toronto Press, 1980.

National Reference Book on Canadian Men and Women. Montreal: Canadian Newspaper Services Ltd., 1936–56.

Neatby, Hilda and Frederick Gibson. *Queen's University*, 2 vols. Kingston: McGill-Queen's University Press, 1978, 1983.

Nett, Emily M. *Canadian Families Past and Present*. Toronto: Butterworths Canada, 1988.

Noel, S.J.R. *Patrons, Clients, Brokers: Ontario Society and Politics, 1791–1896*. Toronto: University of Toronto Press, 1990.

Ontario. Legislative Assembly. *University of Toronto Act*. 1853, 1906, 1947.

Owram, Doug. *Born at the Right Time: A History of the Baby Boom Generation*. Toronto: University of Toronto Press, 1996.

Parker, C.W., ed. *Who's Who and Why*. Vol. 5. Vancouver: International Press Ltd., 1914.

– *Who's Who in Western Canada*. Vancouver: Canadian Press Association, 1911.

Prentice, Alison, et al. *Canadian Women: A History*. Toronto: Harcourt Brace Jovanovich, 1988.

The Presbyterian Church in Canada. *Acts and Proceedings of Assembly*. Toronto, 1876–1996.

Presidents and Professors in American Colleges and Universities. New York: 1935–36.

Prominent People of the Maritime Provinces. St. John, NB: J. and A. McMillan Printers, 1922.

Rae, Bob. *From Protest to Power: Personal Reflections of a Life in Politics*. Toronto: Viking Press, 1996.

Rasky, Harry. *Nobody Swings on Sunday: The Many Lives and Films of Harry Rasky*. Don Mills, ON: Collier Macmillan Canada, 1980.

Ray, Margaret. "What Becomes of the University Woman?" *University of Toronto Monthly* 30 (1929/30): 95–6.

– "What Becomes of the University Woman? Part II." *University of Toronto Monthly* 30 (1929/30): 135–8.

Regehr, T.D. "Elite Relationships, Partnership Arrangements, and Nepotism at Blakes, a Toronto Law Firm, 1858–1942." In *Inside the*

Law: Canadian Law Firms in Historical Perspective, edited by Carol Wilton. Toronto: University of Toronto Press, 1996.

Reid, John G. *Mount Allison University*. 2 vols. Toronto: University of Toronto Press, 1984.

Ridge, Alan D. "C.C. McCaul, Pioneer Lawyer." *Alberta Historical Review* 21 (1973): 21–5.

Ross, Robin. *The Short Road Down: A University Changes*. Toronto: University of Toronto Press, 1984.

Rutherdale, Myra. "Models of Grace and Boundaries of Culture: Women Missionaries on a Northern Frontier, 1860–1940." PhD diss. York University, 1996.

Scholefield, Ethelbert O.S., and Frederic W. Howay, eds. *British Columbia: From the Earliest Times to the Present: Biographical*. Vancouver: S.J. Clarke, 1914.

Schools and Teachers in the Province of Ontario, 1911–1966. Toronto: Media Services and the R.W.D. Jackson Library of the Ontario Institute for Studies in Education, 1985.

Seventy-Five Years of CFUW. Concord, ON: Becker Associates, 1994.

Sibbald, A.S. "The Civil Service as a Career for a University Graduate." *University of Toronto Monthly* 11 (1910/11): 166–72.

Simpson, Lowell. "The Little Republics: Undergraduate Literary Societies at Columbia, Dartmouth, Princeton and Yale, 1753–1865." EdD diss. Columbia University, 1976.

Smyth, Elizabeth, et al. *Challenging Professions: Historical and Contemporary Perspectives on Women's Professional Work*. Toronto: University of Toronto Press, 1999.

Society of Actuaries. *Transactions*. Chicago, 1949–95.

Stamp, Robert M. "Teaching Girls Their 'God Given Place in Life': The Introduction of Home Economics in the Schools." *Atlantis* 2, no. 2, pt. 1 (Spring 1977): 18–34.

Stewart, Lee. *"It's up to you": Women at UBC in the Early Years*. Vancouver: UBC Press, 1990.

"The Literary and Athletic Society – A Fiftieth Anniversary", *University of Toronto Monthly* 4 (1903/04): 135–8.

The Story of the Firm: Clarkson, Gordon and Co., 1864–1964. Toronto: University of Toronto Press, 1964.

Strong-Boag, Veronica. *The New Day Recalled: Lives of Girls and Women in English Canada, 1919–1939*. 2d ed. Toronto: Copp Clark Pitman, 1993.

Thomson, Nancy Ramsay. "The Controversy Over the Admission of Women to University College, University of Toronto." Master's thesis, University of Toronto, 1974.

Ullman, Victor. *Look to the North Star: A Life of William King.* Toronto: Saunders of Toronto, 1969.

United Church of Canada. *Yearbook.* Toronto, 1926–1982.

University College Alumni Directory. Toronto: Harris, 1990.

University College. *Biographical Sketches of the Class of 1915.* Toronto: University of Toronto Alumni House, 1965.

University College Bulletin. Toronto: Registrar's Office of University College, 1960/1–1973.

University College Class of 1883. *Velut arbo aevo: University of Toronto 1883–1933.* Toronto, 1933

University College Class of 1894. *Interesting Facts Regarding the Career of Members of the Arts Class of '94.* Toronto, 1929.

University College Class of 1902. *After Forty Years: Record of the Class of 1902, U.C., in the Forty Years Since Graduation.* Toronto, 1942.

University College Class of 1903. *Those Forty Years 1903–1943, Record of the Class of 1903, University College, University of Toronto, in the Forty Years Since Graduation.* Toronto, 1943.

University College Class of 1914. *Bulletin* 2–3 (1920–1924).

University College Women's Literary Society. *Constitution.* Toronto: Rowsell and Hutchison, 1899.

University of Oxford. *Register of Rhodes Scholars, 1903–1945.* London: Oxford University Press, 1950.

University of Toronto. *Directory of Staff and Students of the University of Toronto and the Federated Colleges.* Toronto, 1928–59.

University of Toronto. *Directory; Students of the University and the Federated Colleges.* Toronto, 1959–66.

University of Toronto. *Register of Graduates.* Toronto: University of Toronto Press, 1920.

University of Toronto Roll of Service, 1914–1918. Toronto: University of Toronto Press, 1921.

University of Toronto Song Book. Toronto: I. Suckling and Sons, 1887.

University of Toronto. *Student Directory.* Toronto, 1967–73.

University of Toronto. *The Yearbook of the University of Toronto.* Toronto: Rowsell and Hutchison, 1887.

Wakelyn, John L. *Biographical Dictionary of the Confederacy*: Westport, CT: Greenwood Press, 1977.

Walden, Keith. "Hazes, Hustles, Scraps and Stunts: Initiations at the University of Toronto, 1880–1925." In *Youth, University, and Canadian Society: Essays in the Social History of Higher Education,* edited by Paul Axelrod and John G. Reid. Montreal: McGill-Queen's University Press, 1989.

Wallace, W.S. *A History of the University of Toronto.* Toronto: University of Toronto Press, 1927.
– "Background." In *University College: A Portrait*, edited by Claude Bissell. Toronto: University of Toronto Press, 1953.
– "The Graduates of King's College, Toronto." *Ontario History* 42 (1950): 163–4.
Westfall, William. "The Divinity 150 Project." Toronto, 1998.
White, Richard. *Gentlemen Engineers: The Working Lives of Frank and Walter Shanly.* Toronto: University of Toronto Press, 1999.
– "Professionals and Academics: Relations Between the School of Practical Science and the University of Toronto, 1878–1906." *Historical Studies in Education* 13 (2001): 147–64.
Who Was Who in America. Chicago: Marquis, 1943– .
Who's Who in Canada. Toronto: International Press, 1911– .
Who's Who in Canadian Law. Toronto: Trans-Canada Press, 1981–87.
Who's Who in Ontario. Vancouver: B+C List, 1996.
Who's Who of Canadian Jewish Women. Downsview, ON: JESL Educational Productions, 1983– .
Who's Who of Canadian Women. Toronto: Trans-Canada Press, 1983– .
Williams, David Ricardo. *Duff: A Life in the Law.* Vancouver: UBC Press, 1984.
Willie, Richard A. "'It is Every Man for Himself': Winnipeg Lawyers and the Law Business, 1870–1903." In *Beyond the Law: Lawyers and Business in Canada, 1830 to 1930*, edited by Carol Wilton. Toronto: The Osgoode Society, 1990.
– *"These Legal Gentlemen": Lawyers in Manitoba, 1839–1900.* Winnipeg: Legal Research Institute of the University of Manitoba, 1994.
Wilton, Carol, ed. *Beyond the Law: Lawyers and Business in Canada, 1830 to 1930.* Toronto: The Osgoode Society, 1990.
– ed. *Inside the Law: Canadian Law Firms in Historical Perspective.* Toronto: University of Toronto Press, 1996.
Wright, Donald A. "The Importance of Being Sexist, or the Professionalization of History in English Canada to the 1950s." Canadian Historical Association, St. John's, NF, 1997.
Young, Clarence Richard, *Early Engineering Education at Toronto, 1851–1919.* Toronto: University of Toronto Press, 1958.

Index